Service Marketing in Ghana
A Customer Relationship Management Approach

Published by
Adonis & Abbey Publishers Ltd & CSED
St James House
13 Kensington Square
London
W8 5HD
Website: http://www.adonis-abbey.com
E-mail Address: editor@adonis-abbey.com

Nigeria:
No. 3, Akanu Ibiam Str.
Asokoro,
P.O. Box 1056, Abuja.
Tel: +234 7066 9977 65/+234 8112 661 609

Year of Publication 2014

British Library Cataloguing-in-Publication Data
A catalogue record for this book is available from the British Library

ISBN: 978-1-909112-48-3

Service Marketing in Ghana
A Customer Relationship Management Approach

John Kuada & Robert Hinson

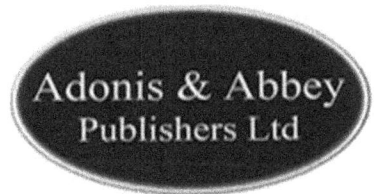

CSED Center for Sustainability and Enterprise Development

Adonis & Abbey Publishers Ltd

TABLE OF CONTENTS

Acknowledgement

The motivation for writing this book comes mainly from Ghanaian managers that we have spoken with during management training sessions and workshops during the past two decades. They have asked us to provide them with guidelines that would enable them to offer services that can improve the performance of their companies and, at the same time, make positive differences in the lives of their customers. This is a daunting task we have taken up in this book. We are, however, aware that no two customers perceive and feel the same way. Thus, managers must always find unique solutions to each customer's problems. What we have tried to do is to offer these managers interesting pointers at sources of solutions that can work.

We are grateful to all the managers who have contributed for providing us with inspiration and insight by sharing their professional experiences with us. We would also like to thank our colleagues in both Ghana and Denmark for their support and critical comments to earlier versions of the manuscript. These discussions have helped us think through some of our arguments and improve the clarity of our thoughts. We are deeply indebted to all of them.

John Kuada
Robert Hinson
June, 2014

This book is dedicated to

Faith Hinson
Esi and Senyo Kuada
for their love and trust

CHAPTER ONE

INTRODUCTION

What to Expect From Reading This Book

1.1 Background and Justification

Just a decade ago, most companies in Ghana considered their products and service offerings to be superior to the market and, therefore, arrogantly ignored their customers. Not any longer. For example, managers within the retail banking sector have realized that their customers are becoming increasingly sophisticated and demanding. The general observation is that as the Ghanaian economy picks up and competition intensifies in most sectors, customers will continue to be more sensitive and less forgiving of the errors that companies make when serving them. They want to be treated with respect and dignity for the money that they pay.

The service sector is one of the very few high growth sectors in the economy. The intensity of competition within the service sector means that marketing managers in the service companies must make extra efforts to satisfy their customers. But what strategies should they adopt to accomplish this and ensure sustainable business performance? This is a question most Ghanaian managers find difficult to answer.

Part of the solution lies in formulating effective customer relationship strategies. It is no longer enough for a Ghanaian service company to be skilful in attracting new customers; it must also retain them and encourage them to recommend the company to their friends and acquaintances. That is, companies must build customer relationships that will prevent their customers from defecting or becoming easy poach-targets.

Chapter One | John Kuada & Robert Hinson
Service Marketing In Ghana
London & Abuja, Adonis & Abbey Publishers and
Center for Sustainability and Enterprise Development (CSED)

The first important step in achieving this goal is to make your customers satisfied with your services. You must be aware that customers tend to express diverse satisfaction or dissatisfaction based on their perceptions of service quality. If the service quality matches with their needs and expectations, they will be satisfied. On the other hand, if the service quality does not fulfil their needs and expectations, they will be dissatisfied and thereby exhibit negative emotions such as regret, anger, and complaints. This means that service quality is an emotional attribute and does not depend only on the service characteristics (objectively defined), but also on customers' relational experiences. Positive emotions such as happiness, pleasure, elation, and a sense of warm-heartedness that customers experience during their interactions with service providers contribute immensely to their overall satisfaction. High performing Ghanaian service providers are becoming increasingly conscious of these marketing facts. Customer relationship management (CRM) is, therefore, capturing the strategic centre stage within the service sector.

1.2 Objectives

This book aims at sharing this awareness with those of you who are managers in your own companies or are employed as managers in service companies in Ghana. The overall objective is to help you remember the basic things that you need to do (or encourage your employees to do) in order for your company to be distinctly and positively in the minds of your customers.

This book is remarkably different from other textbooks you might have come across on the subject. It has the following unique features:

1. We provide you with a state-of-the-art theoretical knowledge in very simple language to facilitate your reading and comprehension.
2. We focus our discussions on the Ghanaian business situation.
3. We provide you with illustrative examples of how some of the Ghanaian companies you are familiar with use the theories

Chapter One | John Kuada & Robert Hinson
Service Marketing in Ghana
London & Abuja, Adonis & Abbey Publishers and
Center for Sustainability and Enterprise Development (CSED)

and ideas in this book in their own marketing practices. These examples are provided in boxes for your quick references.

4. We provide you with suggestions and action points to guide your own strategy formulation. These are also provided in boxes for your quick reference and reflection.

5. We provide you with a number of short cases that reflect the challenges and possible dilemmas that some Ghanaian managers tend to grapple with. The case studies and boxes provide concrete, contemporary examples of the issues involved in various applied settings of service marketing.

Together, these references and action points should hopefully provide you with positive and practically useful learning experiences.

Service marketing's overarching goal is to carefully balance customer acquisition strategies with customer retention strategies. In a simpler language, your job as a manager in a service company is to understand your customers' needs, develop services that provide them with superior customer value, and promote these services effectively so that potential customers will find them attractive enough to pay the price you ask for, simply because they are satisfied with the value that they get. Your relationships with customers will also provide you with new ideas and new ways of enhancing the value of your services and new ways of communicating these values to your customers. It is, therefore, important to encourage your employees to make it a habit to talk to new and regular customers. Create time for them to do so.

Action and Reflection Point 1.2
Treat your Customers as Members of a Royal Family

Your customers are your kings, queens, princes and princesses. They are also your employers. It is because of your customers that your businesses exist. They expect you to make them feel this way. If any of your key customers defects to a competitor, he leaves with a chain of others; if he remains, he brings in a chain of other customers.

Chapter One | John Kuada & Robert Hinson
Service Marketing in Ghana
London & Abuja, Adonis & Abbey Publishers and
Center for Sustainability and Enterprise Development (CSED)

We define a customer in this book as anyone (person or organization) who receives a service from a service provider. In most situations, the customer will have to pay to obtain the service. But this is not always the case. For example, students are increasingly referred to as the 'customers' of schools and colleges that they attend, but the majority of students in public funded schools do not pay directly for the educational service that they receive.

1.3 Key Messages

The key messages in the book include the following:

1. Your performance as a service company manager depends on your ability to assess which customers are worth retaining from a current or potential profitability standpoint and measuring how they react to your offers.
2. Make use of each moment that customers interact with your company to listen carefully to them and bring their voices to bear on your decisions and strategies.

There are many occasions in which a business comes into contact with customers. It is not just about the moment a transaction takes place. Usually, your company will come into contact with its customers in the following situations:

- When a customer is enquiring about the service of your company
- When your company takes a customer order or payment
- When your company delivers a service
- When your company handles a customer's complaint or problem

3. You must adjust your offerings to your customers' needs and be able to manage these offerings better than your competitors so that you can leave your customers with a perception of receiving additional value to the core service you offer.

Chapter One John Kuada & Robert Hinson
Service Marketing in Ghana
London & Abuja, Adonis & Abbey Publishers and
Center for Sustainability and Enterprise Development (CSED)

4. In everything you do, remember that relationships are important. Relationships with all stakeholders must be nursed and stimulated in the right way to stay beneficial to all involved. This requires internal collaboration within your company. Your employees must learn to collaborate within and across departments and also across different areas of responsibility. This will ensure effective service to your customers.

The discussions we present in this book also seek to draw your attention to the impact of certain aspects of the Ghanaian culture on your behaviour as managers (as well as the behaviour of your staff) in relating with your customers. We would like to remind you that many Ghanaian employees take certain patterns of communication and behaviour for granted within and outside their work organizations. But by behaving the way they do, they unknowingly make your customers less satisfied with your services. A classic example is our Ghanaian habit of not saying "thank you" when people buy goods and services from us. Think about this. As children, we are taught by our parents and guardians to say "thank you" when we were offered anything at all. When we grow older we ignore such a basic courtesy. But a simple "thank you" can be all that it takes to win a customer's loyalty for your company.

So, as we reflect on our marketing strategies and customer relations, we must also reflect on the positive and negative rules of behaviour that make us Ghanaians. We may need to make some slight adjustments in our mind-set in order to make our customers and ourselves happier.

In a nutshell, as you go through the pages of this book, we would like you to imagine that your customers are your kings, queens, princes, princesses and bosses. They expect you to make them feel this way. It is because of your customers that your businesses exist. If any of your key customers defects to a competitor, he or she leaves with a chain of others; if they remain, they bring in a chain of other

Chapter One | John Kuada & Robert Hinson
Service Marketing in Ghana
London & Abuja, Adonis & Abbey Publishers and
Center for Sustainability and Enterprise Development (CSED)

11

customers. Highly satisfied customers will stay loyal to your company for a longer period of time. They will also buy more of your services, and will talk favourably about your company and your services and, therefore, encourage potential customers to become your clients. Such customers will also pay less attention to competing brands of services and will be less sensitive to price. So you see, it is good to be nice to every customer you have. In other words, you need to make conscious efforts to build excellent service cultures within your company.

Chapter One | John Kuada & Robert Hinson
Service Marketing in Ghana
London & Abuja, Adonis & Abbey Publishers and
Center for Sustainability and Enterprise Development (CSED)

12

CHAPTER TWO

The Nature of Services and Their Marketing Challenges

2.1 Introduction

We are all customers of service companies and institutions in our private lives. We go to the bank for our financial transactions, to the hospital when we are ill, and to the restaurant on occasions of feeling hungry. We send our children to school and some of us go to the church or mosque for religious purposes. But what is a service? This chapter provides you with some insights into how scholars have described services. The chapter starts with an identification of the key characteristics of services. As a manager, your knowledge of services will help you think more carefully about the marketing strategies that can fulfil your customers' expectations and beat what your immediate competitors can offer. We also discuss the concept of service quality and factors that influence customers' perceptions and expectations of service quality.

2.2 Key Characteristics of Services

What exactly are the characteristics of a service? How are services different from products? Scholars have identified five basic characteristics that distinguish services. These are intangibility, inseparability, heterogeneity, perishability and non-ownership.

Intangibility

Generally speaking, services have limited physical features. It is true that a restaurant is a physical location and the meal you will be served as a customer has physical properties. But the general atmosphere in the restaurant, the time it takes for the meal to be served and the attitude of the employees that you interact with before and during the

Chapter Two | John Kuada & Robert Hinson
Service Marketing in Ghana
London & Abuja, Adonis & Abbey Publishers and
Center for Sustainability and Enterprise Development (CSED)

13

visit all combine to determine your experience of the visit. This intangibility makes it difficult for consumers to evaluate the quality of the services that are delivered to them. It also makes it difficult for service companies to set prices for the values that they deliver and advertise their services in any convincing manner.

Although customer experience is a key determinant of the value of a service, the physical dimensions of a service can, at times, be crucial to the overall service experience of some customers. For example, the physical components of a retail bank service may include architecturally imposing buildings, illuminated signage that welcomes the customer, good quality furniture and fittings, excellent equipment and layouts. For some customers, other tangibles such as letterheads, logos, uniforms, decorations, cheque books and account statement presentations are very important indicators of the quality of the service that the bank delivers to them. In a similar manner, a patient visiting two different hospitals for medical services may be more encouraged to revisit the hospital with a good exterior environment and better designed buildings and landscape rather than a poorly located hospital with dilapidated structures and environment that does not accord with the patient's sense of cleanliness.

Inseparability and Heterogeneity

Each service is unique in a sense, since it is always co-created by a customer and the service provider. Thus, the same meal from a given restaurant may be experienced as tasting differently on different occasions, possibly due to the state of mind of the customer on a given occasion and the attitude of the service personnel on duty on that given day. Thus, once a service is rendered and consumed, it can never be exactly repeated even if the location and assigned resources are the same. The conditions (including the state of life of the service provider and customer) are very likely to change. This means that the moment of service delivery defines the nature and quality of the service and how it will be experienced by the customer.

Chapter Two | John Kuada & Robert Hinson
Service Marketing in Ghana
London & Abuja, Adonis & Abbey Publishers and
Center for Sustainability and Enterprise Development (CSED)

Perishability

Again, while goods are produced first, then stored and sold later, services are produced, sold and consumed at the same time. As such, services cannot be saved, stored, transported, resold or returned. The inability of a service provider to build and maintain stocks means that fluctuations in demand cannot be accommodated in the same way as goods.

Non-Ownership

Unlike physical products, service customers do not secure ownership of the services that they pay for; their payments only secure them access to the services. For example, you pay to use the knowledge of your doctor or lawyer but you do not secure ownership of that knowledge.

The five characteristics described above are likely to pose significant marketing challenges to your company. First, the intangibility of services means that your customers will tend to rely more on subjective impressions in assessing the value of services they receive. This subjective assessment starts immediately customers come into contact with your company – i.e. what is referred to as an initial service encounter. Each time a customer interacts with your company the interaction provides you with an opportunity to give him or her good impression. Second, since the customer cannot judge the quality of the service in advance, the physical dimensions may help define the degree of confidence that the customer is likely to have in your company before approaching it for service delivery. Third, there is a challenge regarding how much of the demand your company should serve profitably and how the demand should be managed. Your company may want to adopt a strategy that encourages excess demand. In this situation, the quality of your services may be below expectation because you are likely to overtax your staff beyond their ability to give consistent service. Equipment and facilities may also be overstretched. To avoid such a situation,

Chapter Two | John Kuada & Robert Hinson
Service Marketing in Ghana
London & Abuja, Adonis & Abbey Publishers and
Center for Sustainability and Enterprise Development (CSED)

your company must strive to have a balanced demand and supply. The dominant characteristics of services are presented in Figure 2.1 for your quick overview.

Figure 2.1 Characteristics of Services

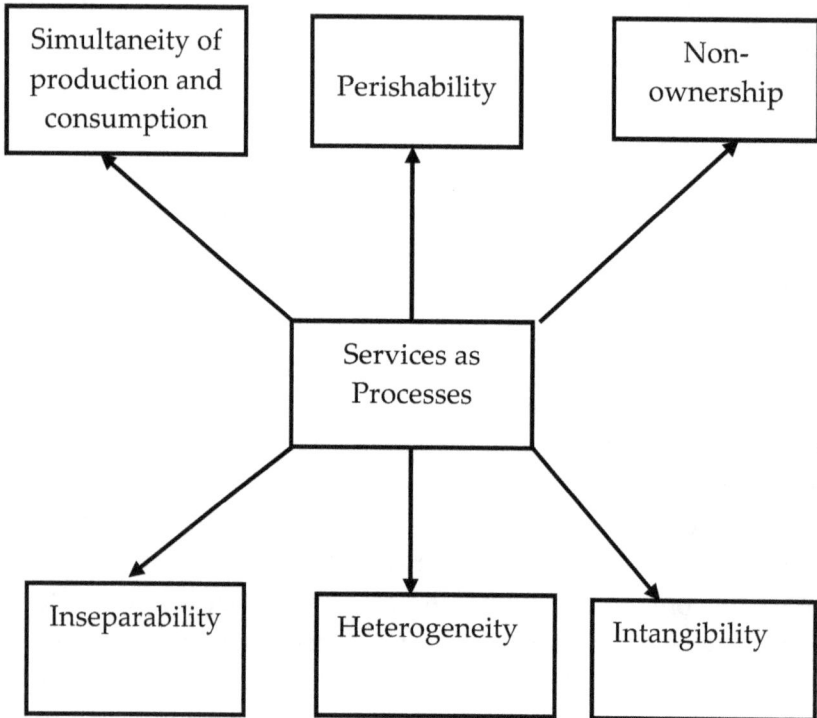

```
┌──────────────────┐   ┌──────────────┐   ┌──────────────┐
│  Simultaneity of │   │              │   │    Non-      │
│  production and  │   │ Perishability│   │  ownership   │
│   consumption    │   │              │   │              │
└──────────────────┘   └──────────────┘   └──────────────┘

              ┌──────────────────┐
              │   Services as    │
              │    Processes     │
              └──────────────────┘

┌──────────────────┐   ┌──────────────┐   ┌──────────────┐
│  Inseparability  │   │Heterogeneity │   │ Intangibility│
│                  │   │              │   │              │
└──────────────────┘   └──────────────┘   └──────────────┘
```

2.3 Service Quality and Customer Perceptions

Understanding consumers' service quality expectations is the key to delivering superior services. Customers tend to compare their service experience with what they expected prior to the delivery in order to determine the quality of the services that they have received. The marketing literature explains this comparison in terms of confirmation / disconfirmation theory. This theory holds that when customers' post-purchase performance of a product or service falls below their pre-purchase expectations, the customer experiences

Chapter Two | John Kuada & Robert Hinson
Service Marketing in Ghana
London & Abuja, Adonis & Abbey Publishers and
Center for Sustainability and Enterprise Development (CSED)

16

negative confirmation and becomes dissatisfied. But when positive disconfirmation occurs (i.e. when the customer expects poor service delivery but experiences a pleasant surprise, he or she becomes pleased and this enhances his/her satisfaction. Customers are, however, mindful of the fact that consistent service delivery is difficult even by the same service employee from one day to another. They are, therefore, willing to accept some variations in service deliveries. Thus, the academic literature defines service quality as the gap between consumer expectations and actual service performance (Parasuraman *et al.*, 1985). It is important to bear in mind that what customers expect may be based on the promises that service companies make in their marketing communications. Your company must, therefore, ensure that you deliver what is promised. Anything short of this will lead to an unsatisfactory service experience. Parasuraman et al. (1988) identified five dimensions of service quality–reliability, responsiveness, assurance, empathy, and tangibility.

Reliability has to do with your company's ability to deliver services within an anticipated time frame. *Responsiveness* refers to the willingness of your employees to help customers. *Assurance* relates to the knowledge and courtesy of your employees and their ability to convey trust and confidence. *Empathy* refers to the provision of caring individualized attention. *Tangibility* here is the same as the physical dimension discussed earlier. Thus, the five dimensions supplement each other to guide you on how you can serve your customers effectively.

You will notice that all the five dimensions can be influenced directly by service employees. Frontline employees directly influence customer perceptions of responsiveness through their personal willingness to help and their promptness in serving customers. Reliability is also very often totally within the control of frontline employees. When services fail or errors are made, employees are those who can set things right, using their judgments to determine the best course of action for service recovery. The assurance dimension of

Chapter Two | John Kuada & Robert Hinson
Service Marketing in Ghana
London & Abuja, Adonis & Abbey Publishers and
Center for Sustainability and Enterprise Development (CSED)

17

service quality is highly dependent on employees' ability to communicate their credibility and to inspire trust and confidence. Empathy implies that employees will pay attention, listen, adapt, and be flexible in delivering what individual customers' need (Zeithaml and Bitner, 2000).

2.4 Customer Service Expectation

Expectation can be defined as the level of service the customer hopes to receive. It is a 'wished for' level – i.e. a combination of what customers believe can and should be delivered in the context of their personal needs. The marketing literature refers to this as a desirable expectation – i.e. reflections of the hopes and wishes of customers. The desirable expectation may also be termed *ideal expectation* – i.e. an expectation of what "perfect" service should be.

However, most customers are realistic and appreciate the fact that companies may not be able to deliver the desired level of service each time, hence they have a tolerance level or "threshold" level of expectations. This is referred to in the marketing literature as the "zone of tolerance" or "adequate service level" – i.e. the range of service performance that customers consider satisfactory. In other words, they may accept some performance variation within that mentally defined range.

Let us take an example that most of you are familiar with. A consumer who buys Malta Guinness on a sunny day expects to be refreshed. But the customer might accept an averagely cold Malta Guinness as adequate service even though he wanted a chilled one. Any increase in performance within this area will only have a marginal positive effect on their perception of the quality of the services that they experience. Only when performance moves outside of this range will it have any real effect on perceived service quality.

Furthermore, the zone of tolerance can increase or decrease for various customers, depending on diverse factors such as competition, price or importance of specific service attributes. These factors most

Chapter Two | John Kuada & Robert Hinson
Service Marketing in Ghana
London & Abuja, Adonis & Abbey Publishers and
Center for Sustainability and Enterprise Development (CSED)

18

often affect adequate service levels much more than desired service levels. For example, if prices increase, customers' zone of tolerance will decrease. That is, adequate service levels move up to close the gap. For example, if you fly first class and the service does not satisfy you, you become less forgiving (because your tolerance zone is decreased). Furthermore, if customers have alternative choices available to them or can provide the service themselves, their levels of adequate service will be higher than those who believe that there are no alternatives to the main service provider.

When customers select a company to deliver the services that they need, they will normally have a prediction of what level of service they are likely to receive based on either of two sets of information/knowledge or a combination of both:

1. Prior experience of customers with a specific service provider, with competing service providers in the same industry, or with related services in different industries.
2. If they have no relevant prior experiences, customers may base their pre-purchase expectation on word-of-mouth comments, news stories, or the service provider's own marketing efforts (mass and non-mass media communication).

Again, these considerations emphasize the importance of customer relations. If you are nice to your customers, they will develop positive emotional attachments to your company and the services that you provide.

2.5 The Kano Model

A well-known marketing model that provides insight into customers' expectations and how to satisfy them is the Kano model. It was created by Professor Noriaki Kano in 1984. The premise of Kano's argument is that not all customer requirements are of equal importance to their assessment of product or service quality. Furthermore, the character and importance of each attribute may vary

Chapter Two | John Kuada & Robert Hinson
Service Marketing in Ghana
London & Abuja, Adonis & Abbey Publishers and
Center for Sustainability and Enterprise Development (CSED)

19

for different market segments. In his view, there are three types of product/service attributes of interest to customers:

Threshold or Basic (i.e. "must have") attributes: Customers expect these attributes to be present in the products and services that they buy. The attributes, however, do not provide an opportunity for service or product differentiation. This means that increasing the performance of these attributes provides diminishing returns in terms of customer satisfaction. But their absence or poor performance will result in extreme customer dissatisfaction. An example of a threshold attribute would be cash in retail banks. For a hospital, the level of competence of doctors and nurses will constitute threshold attributes.

Performance attributes: These are also referred to as discriminators. All other things being equal, more of the attributes increase customer satisfaction. Conversely, the lesser these attributes, the lesser will the customer's satisfaction be. These expectations can be expressed as a linear relationship. For example, a marvellous stereo system and air conditioning in cars increase customer satisfaction besides the threshold attributes of speed, mileage and brakes. If these performance attributes are removed, customer satisfaction will likely diminish. This suggests that once a performance attribute has been included in a product or service, it must be continued. Performance attributes tend to reflect the voice of the customer. The better the product or service in meeting these needs, the happier the customers will be

Excitement attributes (also referred to as attractive dimensions): These are needs that customers themselves are not aware of and therefore do not expect. Their presence can, however, result in high levels of customer satisfaction, although their absence does not lead to dissatisfaction. Thus, excitement attributes often satisfy latent needs – real needs of which customers are currently unaware. In a competitive marketplace where services provide similar performance, offering excitement attributes that address "unknown needs" can

Chapter Two | John Kuada & Robert Hinson
Service Marketing in Ghana
London & Abuja, Adonis & Abbey Publishers and
Center for Sustainability and Enterprise Development (CSED)

20

provide a competitive advantage. An example would be adding extra planes and trains during holiday seasons and taking them off at the end of the holiday season. Bear in mind that some exciter/delighter attributes can become threshold attributes.

As noted above, there is a zone of indifference/tolerance in consumer's expectations and attitudes to these product/service attributes. But the zone of indifference varies with specific customers. Figure 2.2 provides a schematic illustration of the model.

Figure: 2.2: The Kano Model

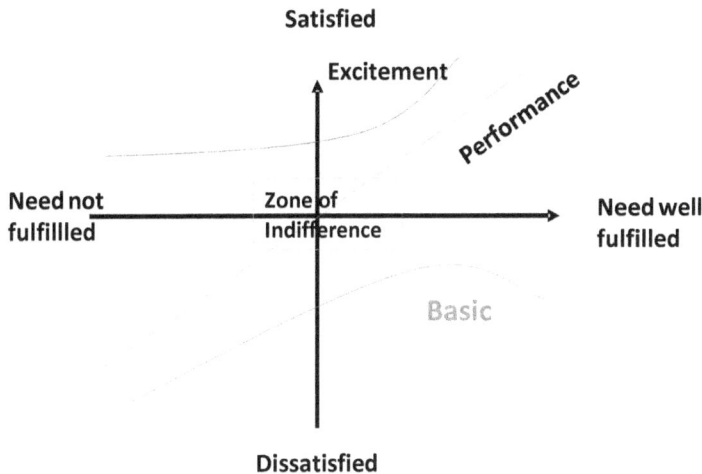

Satisfied

Excitement

Performance

Need not fulfillled

Zone of Indifference

Need well fulfilled

Basic

Dissatisfied

2.6 Summary and Action Points

Take note that as a manager in a service company you cannot provide your customers with superior value without ensuring a close relationship between your customers and your employees who serve them. All services are co-created and their perceived quality depends

Chapter Two | John Kuada & Robert Hinson
Service Marketing in Ghana
London & Abuja, Adonis & Abbey Publishers and
Center for Sustainability and Enterprise Development (CSED)

21

very much on what happens (or is perceived to happen by customers) during the interaction process. Remember further that the importance of various service attributes varies with each customer. But there are always some core service attributes that customers take for granted. There are also performance-enhancing attributes – i.e. those attributes that increase consumers' satisfaction with your services and strengthens their degree of commitment to your company. There are also attributes that are described as "delighters" – i.e. those that provide your consumers with positive surprises and give your services a unique touch. Use this knowledge to design a marketing strategy that can distinguish your company from competing companies. But the main platform for any strategy you formulate will remain the competencies of your employees, their service mind-set and your leadership style. We have developed these ideas further in chapter 4.

At this stage, you must consider these action points:

1. Find out which aspects of the tangible and intangible features of your services your customers consider as: (a) thresholds, (b) discriminatory and performance enhancing, and (c) delighters.
2. Determine how much extra it costs to maintain the delighters to determine if some of them can be ignored for some customer segments.
3. Formulate communication strategies that bring the discriminatory features to the attention of prospective customers.

Chapter Two | John Kuada & Robert Hinson
Service Marketing in Ghana
London & Abuja, Adonis & Abbey Publishers and
Center for Sustainability and Enterprise Development (CSED)

CHAPTER THREE

Putting Your Customers at the Centre of Your Decisions

3.1 Introduction

One of the most recent buzz words in business magazines is *customer-centrism*. A customer-centric approach to business management simply means that the customer is at the centre of all decisions that managers and employees take and the manner in which they behave towards customers. This business philosophy is also described as *market orientation* in academic literature. Market-oriented companies tend to develop business cultures that depend on organisation-wide learning systems. It means all employees continuously learn and reflect over their daily interactions with their customers and share these experiences with other employees through well-organised systems of information generation and sharing. Furthermore, the degrees of customer-orientation shown by employees in their interactions with customers are measured and employees who show higher degrees of customer orientation are rewarded accordingly. In other words, customer-orientation is a key differentiator for businesses today. It means if your company is very customer-oriented it will have sustainable advantage over its immediate competitors.

Thus, your journey to build a strong service company begins with a good understanding of what market orientation is about. This chapter provides you with this insight and shows you how it can help you develop a strong service management culture that can enhance the performance of your company for many years.

The chapter begins with an outline of the dominant characteristics of a market-oriented company in general and market-oriented service companies in particular. This is followed by discussions of the service mind-set concept and its link to market orientation. We also introduce the concepts of market-driven and market driving companies and

Chapter Three | John Kuada & Robert Hinson
Service Marketing in Ghana
London & Abuja, Adonis & Abbey Publishers and
Center for Sustainability and Enterprise Development (CSED)

discuss differences between them. We then relate these concepts to another set of popular concepts in business strategy – i.e. Red ocean and Blue ocean strategies. Thus, the chapter provides you with a new set of business vocabularies that can help you think through the marketing strategies that you may design in order to achieve competitive advantages within your sector.

3.2 Characteristics of a Market-oriented Company

Market oriented companies are those that are highly sensitive to the needs of their customers and proactively take steps to fulfil these needs. Some of the needs may be well articulated by current or potential customers. But there are also occasions where customers are not readily aware of what is technologically possible or how technologies that are soon to be available can fulfil their needs. This means your company must be a step ahead of your customers and suggest new services to them even before they become available on the market. It is this proactive orientation that provides a market-oriented company a sustainable competitive advantage in an increasingly dynamic business environment. It enables such companies to satisfy their **customers better, faster and/or more cheaply than their competitors.**

Market-oriented companies have other defining characteristics. First, they are capable of responding quickly to competitor challenges and are able to spot any evidence of customer dissatisfaction. Second, they will also quickly detect changes in customer needs and product preferences and take the necessary actions in response to the information. Third, they are also effective in getting all business functions to work together to provide superior customer value. Thus, Narver and Slater (1990) perceive market-oriented companies as those that are:

Customer-oriented, i.e. gaining intimate insight into customers' needs and market service requirements;
Competitor-oriented, i.e., gaining understanding of competitors' capabilities and market response patterns; and show a high level of

Chapter Three | John Kuada & Robert Hinson
Service Marketing in Ghana
London & Abuja, Adonis & Abbey Publishers and
Center for Sustainability and Enterprise Development (CSED)

Inter-functional co-ordination, i.e., coordinating the utilization of company resources to create superior customer value

The importance of market information generation as a characteristic of market-oriented businesses has been emphasised by other scholars. For example, Kohli and Jaworski (1990) define market orientation as being composed of three business characteristics:

1. Company-wide generation of market intelligence, pertaining to current and future customer needs.
2. Dissemination of this intelligence among departments of the company.
3. Company-wide response to the knowledge derived from the market intelligence.

In other words, market-oriented firms are expected to gather, interpret and use market information in a more systematic, thoughtful and anticipatory manner than less market-oriented firms.

Building on what we know about high-performing market-oriented businesses, your company can describe itself as truly customer-oriented if it brings the voices of your customers to the centre stage of key decisions. In more practical terms, it means that your company must take deliberate steps to increase its knowledge of its customers. This may be done by requiring all employees that interact with customers to listen attentively to the customers and record the information they provide systematically and share such information with other employees. It also means gathering information systematically from other sources than customers and analysing the information available in the company's database – a process frequently referred to as *data mining*.

Box 3.1 provides excerpts of how the Trust Bank describes itself and its value propositions on its website. It provides some hints about how the company's management understand customer orientation and what service relationships it promises its customers.

Chapter Three | John Kuada & Robert Hinson
Service Marketing in Ghana
London & Abuja, Adonis & Abbey Publishers and
Center for Sustainability and Enterprise Development (CSED)

Box 3.1

Customer Orientation at the Trust Bank

This is an excerpt of what the Trust Bank promises its customers
"Effective customer relationship management is the cornerstone of our Corporate Banking business. It means customer centeredness and tailor made solutions to satisfy the unique needs of each client. We combine our local knowledge with the skills and synergies from our European and African network to achieve this differentiation."

"The customer is at the centre of everything we do. Our product offering is tailored to satisfy the uniqueness of each customer. This means understanding their business or industry, flexibility and capacity to innovate appropriate financial support. We delight our clients with all these and on time."

Available at http://www.trustbank.com.gh/corporatebanking/default.asp Accessed on 12 Sep. 11

3.3 Building a Service Mind-set in your Company

The characteristics of services that we have outlined in chapter 2 indicate that market orientation is extremely important for service companies. Characteristics such as intangibility and co-creation of value (together with customers) suggest that close relationships with customers is essential to any meaningful and effective strategy formulation. Your company, therefore, needs to build a service-oriented mindset among all your employees.

Case 3.1 provides an illustration of how company employees may take initiatives that assuage the irritations that some customers may experience in their interactions with a service provider. They may provide useful lessons to you, particularly with reference to how to train your staff to become more customer-oriented.

Chapter Three | John Kuada & Robert Hinson
Service Marketing in Ghana
London & Abuja, Adonis & Abbey Publishers and
Center for Sustainability and Enterprise Development (CSED)

26

As noted in chapter one, a key point to remember is that there are many occasions on which your business is likely to come into contact with your current or prospective customers. It is not the moment a transaction takes place. Usually, your company will come into contact with your customers in the following situations:

- When a customer is enquiring about the service
- When you take a customer order or payment
- When you deliver a service
- When you handle a customer complaint or problem

The creation of a service mind-set may require the introduction of some structural and procedural changes within your company. You need to decide on what behavioural changes you consider to be necessary and formalize their practice. The concept of formalization is used in management literature to connote the degree to which employees are guided by formal rules and regulations in discharging their responsibilities. Rules can be designed to place the customer at the centre of all business decisions and actions within your company. For example, if your rules mandate employees to meet and discuss matters pertaining to their customers at stipulated intervals or to respond to customer complaints within a specific time frame after receiving the complaints, these rules will naturally lead to higher customer focus within your company. Formal rules are particularly important in Ghanaian companies because many employees are unwilling to take actions on their own for fear of making mistakes. It is a lot easier for them to work according to specific rules.

Formalization can, however, produce some negative side-effects within your company. The management literature is replete with examples in which rule-bound organisations tend to respond less quickly and effectively to changes within their operational environments. Thus, the impact of rules and regulations on market orientation depends both on the nature of the rules and the manner in which they are enforced. This also means that as managers you need to review existing rules and procedures within your company at

Chapter Three | John Kuada & Robert Hinson
Service Marketing in Ghana
London & Abuja, Adonis & Abbey Publishers and
Center for Sustainability and Enterprise Development (CSED)

regular intervals in order to weed out rules that may constrain effective service delivery.

In addition to formalization, you may also need to encourage coordination of customer services within and across departments of your company. Effective coordination implies interdepartmental connectedness which helps remove walls and communication bottlenecks between business functions and build team spirit among your employees. In simpler language, it means that employees must see their colleagues as internal customers and treat them with the same degree of attention, care and empathy as they will treat the external customers of the company. In this way, your customers will experience your service delivery processes to run smoothly, unaware of the multiple decisions and actions that are taken backstage.

But inter-functional coordination does not mean the absence of conflict. Experience has shown that task-related conflicts can be constructive in the sense that they help people recognise problems, identify a variety of solutions and understand the issues involved. Conflicts can, therefore, improve team dynamics by strengthening cohesiveness within your company.

Case 3.1

Service Recovery at Barclays

Eunice opened an account at the Kaneshie branch of Barclays Bank of Ghana limited. She did so because every member of her family had an account with Barclays, and having her own account with the bank would make it easy for her to transfer funds to other family members. On 16th August, 2011, she went to the circle branch to withdraw money from their joint account using the ATM but realized that she did not have her ATM card with her. She decided to do the transaction in the banking hall. She queued for almost thirty minutes before it got to her turn and, to make the waiting extra painful, the cashier made her aware that she could not withdraw the money because the account was a joint one and the mandate on the account was that all the two signatories must sign for all withdrawals. She asked the cashier if she was certain about that explanation because this was not the condition

---

Chapter Three | John Kuada & Robert Hinson
Service Marketing in Ghana
London & Abuja, Adonis & Abbey Publishers and
Center for Sustainability and Enterprise Development (CSED)

28

under which the account was opened. The cashier felt offended and retorted "don't you think I know my job"? She decided to attend to others in the queue, entirely ignoring Eunice. This information proved incorrect when Eunice went to the Kaneshie branch the next day to enquire about the conditions under which her account was opened. This made Eunice even more annoyed and she decided to close her account with Barclays Bank. The third day after the episode at circle branch, Eunice got a call from Doris, another service officer in the Circle branch, who witnessed the episode. She apologized for the manner in which Eunice was treated by her colleague the previous day. Doris offered the apology because she noted that her colleague did not give Eunice the attention that she deserved as a customer and was wondering how Barclays Bank could continue to attract and retain customers if some of her colleagues behaved in such a manner. Eunice thought of reconsidering her decision to close the account, but could not get the nasty treatment she received off her mind.

Questions

1. Why do you think this episode occurred? Why did the cashier behave the way she did?
2. Do you agree with Doris' decision to call and apologise to Eunice?
3. What should management do to avoid such an episode?

3.4 Differences between Market-driven and Market-driving Companies

Marketing scholars draw a distinction between *market-driven* and *market-driving* companies. This distinction is useful in your understanding of the roles that your company currently plays within the market, how customers perceive its service offerings and what strategies it can adopt in order to sustain its competitive position and ensure superior performance.

If your company is *market-driven*, it means it is market-oriented in a conventional sense. As we have explained in the previous section, such a company has a good understanding of its current and potential customers' needs and is capable of attracting and keeping them by

Chapter Three | John Kuada & Robert Hinson
Service Marketing in Ghana
London & Abuja, Adonis & Abbey Publishers and
Center for Sustainability and Enterprise Development (CSED)

satisfying these needs better than other companies. This requires gathering, analysing and disseminating customer information throughout the company to ensure that all employees have the same information about the key customers and can therefore serve them effectively.

Managers in a market-driven company assume that customers have full knowledge of their needs and are willing to reveal these needs when asked about them. The strategy of companies managed with such an assumption can be described mainly as reactive – i.e. reacting effectively to declared customer needs. To do so, the company must possess distinctive capabilities and resource configuration which allows it be agile – i.e. adapt swiftly to changing customer needs (Day, 1999).

Remember that there is a difference between building a market-driven (or customer-oriented) service culture in your company and becoming a *customer-compelled* service company. The marketing literature describes customer-compelled companies as those which bend over backwards to whatever customers want, trying to be everything for every single customer. In their zeal to be customer-oriented, they are unable to focus and discipline their marketing strategies. Marketing costs increase more than the customer values they deliver, leading to low profitability. This is bad management. It may lead to the collapse of your company thereby making your customers, employees, shareholders and yourself losers.

As we noted earlier, many top companies in Ghana are emphasising customer orientation as the foundation of their strategies. An example of such a company is Toyota Ghana. Box 3.2 provides some excerpts from the company's website indicating its desire to be seen by its customers as customer-focused.

A new version of market orientation suggests that high performing companies can be *market driving* (rather than market-driven). Your company may be described as market driving if your top managers base the company's strategies on a different view about customers. They are likely to make two sets of implicit assumptions.

Chapter Three | John Kuada & Robert Hinson
Service Marketing in Ghana
London & Abuja, Adonis & Abbey Publishers and
Center for Sustainability and Enterprise Development (CSED)

First, they will assume that not all customers know exactly what they need at any given point in time. This means market research will not always reveal what customers are likely to buy. The second possible assumption is that most customers prefer companies that provide them new products and services and help them know about the value additions that the products can provide them. That is, the successes of such companies as Google, Facebook and Starbuck have been attributed to their market-driving strategies. Databank Group may also be considered an example of a Ghanaian service company that has successfully adopted market-driving strategies. (See case 3.2)

If your company's strategies are guided by these assumptions, it is likely to re-define the rules of the "business game", rather than try to be barely better at the old game (as a market-driven company is likely to do). This means that your role as a marketing manager is entirely different in a market driving company. It becomes one of teaching customers what they want rather than providing them with what they think they want. Your company's strategies will, therefore, produce sustainable competitive advantages not because the company is satisfying customers better, faster and/or more cheaply than their competitors. But because customers perceive what your company is providing as novel and more value-adding. In other words, your company can be both expensive and competitive at the same time.

Box 3.2

Customer Orientation at Toyota Ghana Company Limited

You will find the following message Toyota Ghana's website:

Our Customer Service Department was set up in line with our motto, 'A satisfied customer, Our Pride'. Its goal is to continually improve the services we render to our customers and give them an official office to send their concerns and have a speedy and satisfying redress. The main activities of the department are:

Chapter Three | John Kuada & Robert Hinson
Service Marketing in Ghana
London & Abuja, Adonis & Abbey Publishers and
Center for Sustainability and Enterprise Development (CSED)

31

- Customer Complaint Handling
- Conducting Research (Survey)
- Conducting Post-Service follow-up

Customer Complaint Handling

- All TGCL workers are trained in the art of good customer relations. Our workers believe in the philosophy that "the customer is always right". That is what we preach and practice.
- Staff members have been appointed in all our departments to see to the administration of good customer service.
- There are regular meetings of CS representatives from the various departments to deliberate on current complaints and find ways of satisfying the customers involved.
- CS representatives have access to modern client/server applications through which they can receive, book and assign complaints received.

Conducting Research (Survey)

- We do customer survey by phone or visits for all operational departments (Sales, Service, BP, Part, Kumasi)
- Our current Customer Satisfaction Index (CSI) is 72.9%. We also conduct post survey follow ups.

Available at: http://www.toyotaghana.com/cs-cust-service.html Accessed on 11 September, 2011

3.5 Dual Market-oriented Strategies

Note that to be truly market-oriented in a rapidly changing marketplace, your company must be both market-driven and market-driving. This means you must pursue a dual market-oriented strategy. In other words, some of your strategic initiatives must be proactive while the others may be reactive. This dual market-oriented strategy is captured in a popular model by Boston Consulting Group found in most marketing textbooks – usually referred to as the BCG

Chapter Three | John Kuada & Robert Hinson
Service Marketing in Ghana
London & Abuja, Adonis & Abbey Publishers and
Center for Sustainability and Enterprise Development (CSED)

32

model. It classifies a company's products or service offerings into four main categories as shown in Figure 3.1:

Figure 3.1: **The Boston Matrix**

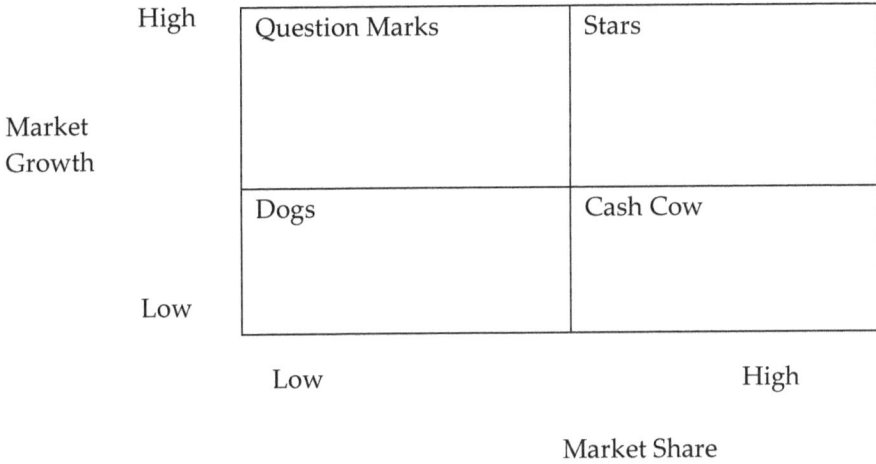

	Low	High
High	Question Marks	Stars
Market Growth		
	Dogs	Cash Cow
Low		

Low   High

Market Share

Let us take a quick look at what these categories cover and the implications they carry for your marketing strategy formulation.

Stars

These are your new/innovative services that provide values that your customers did not anticipate. They create a new business area for you and give you a first mover advantage in this business. As long as you can hold competitors off, your compnay can establish itself effectively in that business area. Continuous renewal should ensure you a strong position. This, therefore, becomes your market-driving territory.

But take note that your company is a pioneer in this line of business and your potential customers have no knowledge of how valuable the service is. Many of them will, therefore, show substantial uncertainties about deciding to try it. In other words, your marketing strategy must emphasise persuasion – i.e. encouraging the customers

Chapter Three | John Kuada & Robert Hinson
Service Marketing in Ghana
London & Abuja, Adonis & Abbey Publishers and
Center for Sustainability and Enterprise Development (CSED)

33

to give the service a try. It means that, customers must be taught what the service can do for them and be provided justification for making the first choice.

Cashcows

These are goods and services that customers are familiar with and demand. Market-driven companies that are successful with their marketing strategies usually have high market shares of the types of services. They are also able to make profit in these businesses due to their superior ability to serve their customers.

Question Marks

Question mark products and services are also known as *problem children*. They are classified as such because they have shown disappointing performances on the market. You need to find out the reasons for the poor performance and take appropriate actions to strengthen the market acceptability of this service. A question mark has the potential to gain market share and become a star, and eventually a cash cow when the market growth slows. Note that if you classify any of your services as a question mark and do not succeed in turning it into a market leader, then after perhaps years of cash consumption it will degenerate into a dog when the market growth declines.

Dogs

Dogs are services that are no longer in high demand and you will need to spend more to serve your customers than they are willing to pay. It is always advisable to phase out such services quickly or re-launch them as new services to new target customers who will see it as kind of "star". If your company has competencies in re-innovating your services in this way, it will sustain its competitive position in this market for a long period of time.

Chapter Three | John Kuada & Robert Hinson
Service Marketing in Ghana
London & Abuja, Adonis & Abbey Publishers and
Center for Sustainability and Enterprise Development (CSED)

Let us consider the Ghanaian retail sector as an illustrative example of dual market-oriented service strategy. The sector is currently split between two polarised market segments – the low end segment such as Makola and Agbogbloshi markets on the one hand, and the high end segment represented by Accra Mall. The mid-market segment remains unexplored despite the growing middle income consumer group in the country. A company that provides retail services appealing to this segment of consumers will be driving the market segment rather than be driven by it. But if you are in the retail business you can provide improved value to existing consumers at Agbogbloshie. Think of a solar driven cold store system or warehouse where traders can keep their fresh fruits, vegetables and foodstuffs, going for new consignments from the cold store only after selling the quantities on their stalls. This will be considered significant service improvement in such a marketplace.

Case 3.2
The Story of Databank Group

Databank was established in 1990 by three Ghanaians Ken Ofori-Atta, Keli Gadzekpo and James Akpo. It started its operations from a small room in the UTC building in Central Accra with a short term (money market) loan of US$25,000. Its initial goal was to compile and collate research data for the financial sector and the emerging capital market. It quickly became a useful source of information on the Ghanaian stock market which started its operation about the same time by computing and publishing the first indices the *Databank Stock Index* (DSI) and *Databank Stock Average* (DSA). This became the only reliable performance measures until the Ghana Stock Exchange was able to compute its own index the GSE All-Share Index from 1994. The three entrepreneurs, therefore, identified a service gap within the emerging financial sector and created a service package that could serve potential customers even before the industry as a whole became aware of the importance of these services.

Databank has evolved into a full-service investment banking firm offering stock brokerage, corporate finance, asset management, equity research and

---

Chapter Three | John Kuada & Robert Hinson
Service Marketing in Ghana
London & Abuja, Adonis & Abbey Publishers and
Center for Sustainability and Enterprise Development (CSED)

35

private equity services. The company has established distinctive but complementary strategic business units which include Databank Brokerage Ltd. (DBL), Databank Asset Management Services Ltd. (DAMSEL), Databank Financial Services Ltd., (DFS), Databank Private Equity (DPE) Ltd., Databank Research and Information Ltd. (DRIL), and Databank Client Services (DCS) Ltd., each run by its own Executive Director. It now has its own corporate headquarters and three country subsidiaries – Databank Securities Ltd. in The Gambia, Sierra Leone and Liberia. The vision is to emerge as a Regional investment bank with a primary focus on asset management and other investment banking services. The company has also set the pace for financial journalism by publishing regular features and articles that now shape the financial policy and strategy agenda in the country.

Each of these business units has been at the forefront of the development of new investment services in Ghana. For example, DAMSEL started the first licensed mutual fund in Ghana EPACK. From a modest beginning of an initial 250,000 Cedis from five people in 1996, EPACK has grown to over 330 billion Cedis and over 40,000 shareholders as at October 2006, a growth of over 5,600% over the period. Currently, EPACK is probably the only Pan African Mutual Fund on the African continent, investing in Ghana, Nigeria, South Africa, Botswana, Kenya, Mauritius, Zambia and Malawi. There are plans to invest in the buoyant Egyptian and Tunisian markets. In 2004, DAMSEL also licensed the first fixed income (money market) mutual fund M Fund, another industry first.

The CEO attributes Databank's success to its customer-centric business philosophy. He is quoted as saying "Our overriding goal and strategy is to ensure that the Databank Group keeps faith with our commitment to give gold standard customer service. That our customers, present and potential, deserve the very best from our staff is not negotiable".

Based on an article from
http://www.gipc.org.gh/gc100/article_databank.asp

Accessed on 11.09.11

Chapter Three | John Kuada & Robert Hinson
Service Marketing in Ghana
London & Abuja, Adonis & Abbey Publishers and
Center for Sustainability and Enterprise Development (CSED)

3.6 Red Ocean and Blue-Ocean Service Companies

As noted above, a market-oriented company is one that adopts both proactive and reactive strategies – i.e. focuses on matching and beating its rivals and at the same time exploring new business terrains. The reactive parts of its strategy are basically concerned with designing capabilities that enable the company to engage in head-to-head competition based largely on incremental improvements in cost and quality, or both within the prevailing market space. But as the market space gets crowded, prospects for profits and growth are reduced, and cut-throat competition drains the energy of individuals and their entire organisations. The proactive component of the market-oriented strategy is what we label as market driving. This encourages the company to innovate and find new market spaces.

In 2005 W. Chan Kim and Renée Mauborgne from INSEAD published the book *Blue Ocean Strategy - How to Create Uncontested Market Space and Make Competition Irrelevant*. It quickly became a best seller because it provided a new strategic direction to many managers. The arguments and illustrative cases in the book provide additional evidence in support of the dual market-oriented strategy presented above.

Kim and Mauborgne based their views on years of investigations of the strategic orientation of different firms in different industries. Their study showed that the strategic thinking of less successful firms was dominated by the idea of staying ahead of the competition by using market-driven strategies. In stark contrast, the high-growth companies paid little attention to matching or beating their rivals. Instead, they sought to make their competitors irrelevant through a strategic logic that they called *value innovation*. That is, value innovative companies create products or services for which there are no direct competitors. In this way, they break free from their competitors by going beyond the existing service boundaries in order to create new market space.

Chapter Three | John Kuada & Robert Hinson
Service Marketing in Ghana
London & Abuja, Adonis & Abbey Publishers and
Center for Sustainability and Enterprise Development (CSED)

37

They then developed the terms *red* and *blue oceans* to provide a symbolic picture of the contrasts in the strategic orientations of the consistently successful and less successful firms. Red oceans are all the industries in existence today - the known market space. In red oceans, industry boundaries are defined and accepted, and the competitive rules of the game are known. Blue oceans, in contrast, represent all the industries not in existence today – i.e. unknown market space untainted by competition. In blue oceans, demand is created rather than fought over, and there is ample opportunity for growth.

They argued that the creation of blue oceans is a result of proactive strategy and managerial action. Thus, businesses that aspire to sustain their competitive advantages must be consistently engaged in strategic moves that create new blue oceans since competitors are always ready to crowd into new markets by imitating best practices of the value innovators.

Blue ocean strategy, therefore, requires a different competitive mind-set and a systematic way of looking for opportunities. Instead of searching within the conventional boundaries of industry competition, managers can look methodically across those boundaries to find unoccupied territory that represents real value innovation.

Kim and Mauborgne offer the following guidelines to firms in the blue ocean strategy formulation process:

1. Do not compete in existing market space instead you should create uncontested market space.
2. Do not beat the competition instead you should make the competition irrelevant.
3. Do not exploit existing demand instead you should create and capture new demand.
4. Do not make the value/cost trade-off instead you should break the value/cost trade-off.

As we noted earlier, making new product/service offering involves more than simply "getting close to the customer". It entails

Chapter Three | John Kuada & Robert Hinson
Service Marketing in Ghana
London & Abuja, Adonis & Abbey Publishers and
Center for Sustainability and Enterprise Development (CSED)

being a step ahead of your customers and completely understanding the market in order to be able to reconstruct the customer value attributes. When the founders of Facebook created the site, they were engaged in blue ocean strategy simply because it was a new site that served a purpose no other site did. During its early years of growth, Facebook continued to rollout new features that no one else had thought of -- business pages, linking to other websites, like button, and check-ins, to name a few. This strategy was meant to expand the new market space and make it attractive to new and existing customers through value additions.

Marketing scholars have observed that customers may not always provide useful information for business strategy formulations. This is because when asked about their wants, customers lack imagination to suggest radical changes in products. Furthermore, consumers act highly rationally within some set of false beliefs resulting in buying predictions that may not be validated by subsequent actions. Thus, businesses cannot fully understand the needs of their customers by asking them, since most customers may not have imaginations stretching beyond their immediate circumstances. By thinking with customers and reaching beyond their immediate requirements, businesses are engaged in creating new markets for themselves by offering values that enable their customers to create new markets themselves. This is what the concept of co-creation is about.

The discussions so far suggest that your company can sustain its competitive position for many decades into the future if you change the mindset of your management and your employees from being less customer-oriented to being more customer-focused. Your company will then be characterized as being market-oriented. Your strategic orientation must be both proactive and reactive. The reactive strategies respond to explicitly articulated customer needs, while the proactive strategies seek to explore hitherto unknown business opportunities through value innovation.

Successful value innovation must be stakeholder-friendly and must have a compelling "value proposition" for buyers, a "profit

Chapter Three | John Kuada & Robert Hinson
Service Marketing in Ghana
London & Abuja, Adonis & Abbey Publishers and
Center for Sustainability and Enterprise Development (CSED)

39

proposition" for companies and a "people proposition" for employees and partners. It is this whole-system approach, integrating a firm's functional and operational activities, that makes the creation of blue oceans a sustainable strategy.

Kim and Mauborgne's work has been very much praised as nothing more than an excellent marketing endeavour, based on the originality and intrigue of its title and subtitle as well as the introduction of captivating new labels. But, on the whole, it is a combination of several old concepts and views expressed by many other authors (Gandellini, and Venanzi, 2011). But it certainly provides new perspectives of the previously well-known concepts. Furthermore, it offers a comprehensive systematization of the strategic process that allows the identification and exploitation of new industry sectors and market spaces.

3.7 Purple Ocean Strategies and Interface Management

The BCG model presented above (Figure 3.1) classifies products and services into four main categories. This neat categorization may not always be easy in practice. At any given point in time some products and services may find themselves in transitional stages, moving in-between the cells. For example, companies may find some of their services being considered as stars by some segments of the market while other segments may consider them question marks. The main strategic challenge for companies is how to manage these interfaces between the cells when the services cannot neatly fit into any category.

This challenge is addressed by some recent writers by extending Kim and Mauborgne's blue ocean concept and suggesting the formulation of *purple ocean strategies*. Purple ocean strategies are supposed to combine some of the characteristics of the red-ocean and blue ocean strategies. What happens in practice is that competitors quickly discover the new business opportunity presented by a blue ocean company and quickly erode the first mover-advantages created. The company, therefore, needs to engage in incremental

Chapter Three | John Kuada & Robert Hinson
Service Marketing in Ghana
London & Abuja, Adonis & Abbey Publishers and
Center for Sustainability and Enterprise Development (CSED)

40

innovative practices in order to extend the duration of these advantages. These incremental strategies can very well be described as purple ocean-oriented.

We have suggested above that the establishment of Facebook was a clear example of blue ocean strategy. But aspects of Facebook's strategies are not entirely blue ocean-oriented. The company has in some regard been battling with competitors by creating features that it claims are "unrelated" to other networks, despite the fact that those features serve a need other platforms already supplied. Facebook, today, is therefore engaged more in purple ocean strategies than blue-ocean strategies.

The message here is that your company must not strive to create an uncontested market space if it does not have the capabilities to do so. It can improve its performance and sustain its competitive advantages by adopting purple ocean strategies and minimizing its need to engage in frontal attacks with its major competitors. A smart strategy is one of cost-effective incremental innovations – i.e. give your customers a feeling of "newness" in your existing services, a value that they will be willing to pay for.

3.8 Summary and Action Points

1. Remember that the first step in getting your customers to like your company is to demonstrate that your company and employees like them. It is, therefore, important that you make your company customer-focused.

2. Whenever you take a business decision always ask yourself "what will our customers think of this particular decision? How will it affect their perceived value of the services we offer them?

3. Being customer-focused means adopting twin marketing strategies – market driven and market driving strategies. That is, you must create something new and at the same time respond effectively to the declared needs of your customers.

Chapter Three | John Kuada & Robert Hinson
Service Marketing in Ghana
London & Abuja, Adonis & Abbey Publishers and
Center for Sustainability and Enterprise Development (CSED)

CHAPTER FOUR

Challenges to Customer-Oriented Business Culture in Ghana

4.1 Introduction

As hinted earlier, it is the frontline employees that influence customers' perceptions of a service company's responsiveness to their needs. They do so through their personal willingness to go the 'extra mile' to serve their customers (or annoy them with their bad work attitude). This means that whether or not a customer perceives a company as delivering the service promised depends on the attitude, commitment and behaviour of service employees. The management literature shows that work attitude is partly shaped by organizational culture. This means a customer service environment should have a customer service-oriented culture. As Narver and Slater (1990) explain it, customer-orientation is nothing less than an organisational culture which enlists the participation of all employees for purposes of creating superior value for a company's customers and superior performance for itself.

We have earlier indicated that such a culture is rather rare in Ghana. This means that existing cultural attributes in organisations can act as a barrier to the effective implementation of market-oriented tools and behaviours. Following this thinking, Ghanaian service companies must "unlearn" their non-market oriented behaviour and replace them with market-oriented values, attitudes and practices.

In this chapter, we draw your attention to how Ghanaian customers feel about their service providers and explain how the most frequent causes of annoyance may be found in some of our culturally endorsed rules of behaviour. We then provide you with guidelines for how you can create a customer-focused service culture within your company.

Chapter Four | John Kuada & Robert Hinson
Service Marketing in Ghana
London & Abuja, Adonis & Abbey Publishers and
Center for Sustainability and Enterprise Development (CSED)

4.2 How Ghanaian Customers Feel about their Service Companies

Annoyances, nuisances, frustrations and anything that upsets a customer may be termed *service irritations*. These irritations range from minor issues that the customer can easily overlook to major blunders that cause the customer to cut all business links with your company. This is even more prominent where the contacted employee is the 'service' in the eyes of the customer. For example, customers see a consultant, a teacher, and a nursing officer as the service and so any service blunder they commit directly affects the customers' decision to patronise the services of the provider.

We did a focus group study recently about what ordinary Ghanaian customers find irritating with their service providers. The top 6 concerns raised are consistent with those found in the service marketing literature. They are listed in box 4.1:

Box 4.1
Top Six Moments of Irritation to Ghanaian Customers

1. Employees failing to show up to appointments.
2. Poorly informed employees do not have good answers for customers' queries.
3. Employees on personal phone calls while customers wait to be served.
4. Talking down to customers
5. Robotism
6. Rule-based behaviour

Let us take a closer look at each of them.

7. Personnel Failing to Show up to Appointments

Customers find it highly irritating when they turn up for business transactions and do not meet personnel who are to attend to them.

Chapter Four │ John Kuada & Robert Hinson
│ *Service Marketing in Ghana*
│ London & Abuja, Adonis & Abbey Publishers and
│ Center for Sustainability and Enterprise Development (CSED)

Take this example: You run an equipment service company and one of your clients calls in for a piece of equipment in his office to be serviced. The servicing is scheduled for a given day and time. You send one of your service technicians to the client but he fails to turn up at the appointed time, fails to give the client a call that he will be delayed, and fails to communicate through any other available means. After four hours of waiting, the technician shows up with a smile on his face and no apology. How would you expect your client to feel?

8. Poorly Informed Providers

Customers naturally expect employees to be so well informed that they can address all customer complaints and queries to them. This does not appear to be the case. For example, a helpdesk attendant of a Ghanaian telecommunication company was asked about the rate per minute for overseas calls. The attendant asked for time to find out. One would have expected a telephone charge sheet to have been made available to this attendant for reference. This kind of situation causes customers to doubt the general level of knowledge of other employees in the firm. Thus, a customer's perception of the company is severely affected, leading to a potential loss of customers.

9. Employees on Personal Phone Calls while Customers Wait

In this age of mobile telephone, it is common in Ghana to see customers queuing for a service while the contacted employee who is to serve them engages in a telephone conversation that has nothing to do with the job. Such behaviours may be tolerated in markets where competition is nearly absent. As we noted above, the nature of competition and the degree of customer sophistication in Ghana has changed significantly over the past three decades. Many Ghanaians now travel to other parts of the world where they experience other service quality levels. This has narrowed the zone of their tolerance significantly.

Chapter Four | John Kuada & Robert Hinson
Service Marketing in Ghana
London & Abuja, Adonis & Abbey Publishers and
Center for Sustainability and Enterprise Development (CSED)

45

10. Talking Down to Consumers

Some Ghanaian employees do not seem to appreciate the fact that they are in employment because of customers or that their customers are doing them a favour by patronizing their services. Commonly cited examples are utility services employees in companies such as the Electricity Company of Ghana, Ghana Water Company and Ghana Telecom (GT). Some customers have complained about the staff of these companies talking down to them when all they wanted were reasons why they were not getting the services they had paid for.

11. Robotism

Some customers feel that they are sometimes treated like inputs into a system that must be processed. In other words, the customers do not feel that their views are considered when decisions concerning them are taken. A frequently cited example is in the consultation rooms of Ghanaian medical officers. Ghanaian doctors are reputed for not taking time to interact with their patients and to explain to them what their illnesses are and what implications the illnesses may have for them. When a doctor talks to a patient, he or she does so condescendingly.

12. Rule-based Behaviour

Customers feel that service providers are not adequately empowered to take decisions that ensure effective service delivery. In many service organizations, the rules laid down to guide employees in their work and their relationships with customers have become obstacles to innovations in their service delivery. Employees are more likely to live by the rules to the detriment of customers even if the rules do not make sense.

We have earlier suggested that you must treat your customers as if they were members of a royal family. We have also noted that some Ghanaian companies are beginning to develop deliberate customer-

Chapter Four | John Kuada & Robert Hinson
Service Marketing in Ghana
London & Abuja, Adonis & Abbey Publishers and
Center for Sustainability and Enterprise Development (CSED)

46

oriented strategies. But occasionally, managers face the dilemma of accepting some customer complaint if such a move can increase costs substantially or have long term negative implications on the company's operations. Case 4.1 provides you with an illustrative example of such a situation.

Case 4.1

Fiasco at the Fiesta Royale Hotel

Beginning with its profile, the Fiesta Royale Hotel, which is owned by a Ghanaian, started as Cresta Royale Hotel in 2003 and later changed to its present name in 2005. The hotel presently has 230 employees including a manager. Located five minutes away from Ghana's main airport, the Kotoka International Airport in Accra, and 15 minutes away from the Accra city centre, Fiesta Royale Hotel is one of the hotels of choice for travellers and business conferences. Mr. Fred Williams, the newly appointed managing director of Fiesta Royale Hotel, has been confronted with an issue which could put his job on the line and the organization in a bad light, if not handled properly. A potential business partner, who arrived from the USA to sign a conference deal, encountered a theft issue, which he is demanding a fair hearing and solution to. The management is reluctant to accept responsibility and the potential customer has lodged a formal complaint, threatening to sue the Hotel and also send the case to the press. This has set the manager in a quandary as it could also lead to a loss of opportunity this particular deal could bring, should things go the way it is going.

Questions

1. Should the hotel accept responsibility and pay off the client? Why?
2. Should the hotel call-off the bluff of the client and accept the consequences? Why?
3. How can such service failures be avoided?

Chapter Four | John Kuada & Robert Hinson
Service Marketing in Ghana
London & Abuja, Adonis & Abbey Publishers and
Center for Sustainability and Enterprise Development (CSED)

47

4.3 Cultural Explanations of Weak Service Performance

We have noted that the reasons why some Ghanaian employees appear to show blatant disregard for customers' needs and emotions may be partly found in the Ghanaian culture. Culture is usually described as a system of socially transmitted behaviour patterns that serve to relate human communities to their environment as well as order relations among individuals. The transmission mechanism is referred to as the process of socialization. Through socialization, individuals are taught the norms and values as well as the shared expectations of the community in which they live. The process starts from childhood. Each child is taught the customs and norms of "good behaviour" of a particular sub-unit of its community in order to equip it with the means of interacting sensibly and smoothly within the community. As the child grows older, other members of the community become involved in the transmission mechanism to build him/her into a useful citizen of the community.

Hofstede (2001) describes culture in terms of six dimensions:

Power distance - indicating the extent to which a society accepts the fact that power in institutions and organizations is distributed unequally. The distribution of power in a society is reflected in the values of both the less powerful and the more powerful members of the society.

Uncertainty avoidance - indicating the extent to which a society feels threatened by uncertain and ambiguous situations and tries to avoid these situations by providing clearly defined rules to guide peoples' behaviour. Uncertainty avoidance may create a strong inner urge in people to work hard in order to protect themselves against eventualities in the future.

Individualism - Collectivism - indicating whether the social framework in which people are supposed to take care of themselves

Chapter Four | John Kuada & Robert Hinson
Service Marketing in Ghana
London & Abuja, Adonis & Abbey Publishers and
Center for Sustainability and Enterprise Development (CSED)

48

is loosely or tightly knit. Individualistic societies are loosely knit while collectivistic societies are believed to be tightly knit.

Masculinity - Femininity - indicating the extent to which the dominant values in the society is characterized by assertiveness, acquisition of money etc. (masculinity) or emphasizes quality of life, sympathy and support for the disadvantaged (femininity).

Long-term and Short-term Orientation – describing how people in a given society relate to time. People in long term oriented societies attach more importance to the future. They foster pragmatic values oriented towards rewards - emphasizing persistence, saving and capacity for adaptation. In short terms, oriented societies' values promoted are related to the past and the present, including steadiness, respect for tradition, and the fulfilment of social obligations.

Indulgence versus Restraint – Indulgence stands for a society that allows relatively free gratification of basic and natural human drives related to enjoying life and having fun. Restraint stands for a society that suppresses gratification of needs and regulates it by means of strict social norms.

Seen from the Hofstedian perspective, the Ghanaian culture may be characterized as having high power distance, high degree of uncertainty avoidance, moderately masculine, highly short term-oriented, and moderately indulgent in immediate pleasures. Some see the Ghanaian culture as collectivistic. These dominant cultural characteristics help explain our attitude to time, acceptance of rule-bound behaviours, talking down to people we feel superior to, ignoring the immediate needs of non-kin members of our society, and exhibiting limited self-sacrifice in our relations with others.

Let us take our attitude to time as an example. We all know that time passes by without notice in Ghana or is simply ignored. You do not expect a person to arrive on the time given on an invitation. If he finally

Chapter Four | John Kuada & Robert Hinson
Service Marketing in Ghana
London & Abuja, Adonis & Abbey Publishers and
Center for Sustainability and Enterprise Development (CSED)

49

does, do not expect an apology. He has arrived, and that is what matters.

Box 4.2
Ghanaian Attitude to Time

"It is very much like us (Ghanaians) to wait till a day is left before we go to the dressmaker to be measured for the dress we want tomorrow. Naturally, the dress is not usually ready when the next day comes. What may have happened is that another customer came after us; his tomorrow sounded more urgent, he had more to offer for incentives, and stood guard over the dressmaker to ensure that he applied himself/herself to the work in hand. One customer who could not mount guard called for collection a whole week after the date given him, but still went away empty-handed. To his complaints, the dressmaker replied, asking, why he did not come when told?" Daniels (1993:19)

A renowned Ghanaian sociologist Assimeng (1981) describes a Ghanaian as being characterized by:

1. Conformity and blatant eschewing of individual speculations
2. Unquestioning acquiescence
3. Lack of self-reliance, owing to the pervading influence of the extended family system
4. Fetish worship of authority and charismatic leaders
5. Hatred for criticism

As Daniel (1993) writes "we are law-abiding, brought up to be. There are children who dutifully fetch the cane to be whipped! They grow up to be good Ghanaians. Often, during national emergencies especially, announcements come on the air for people to report to the nearest police station to be detained. The good Ghanaian complies." With such a personality profile, many Ghanaians will be hesitant to alter situations that they find unfavourable, if their actions will involve substantial risk to themselves. For most of us, failing to act is less risky than acting and failing.

Chapter Four | John Kuada & Robert Hinson
Service Marketing in Ghana
London & Abuja, Adonis & Abbey Publishers and
Center for Sustainability and Enterprise Development (CSED)

But the Ghanaian culture has experienced some significant changes over the years. For example, there is an increasing tendency among Ghanaians to adopt individualistic and opportunistic attitude to life in general. Disregard for collective rules and codes of conduct are emerging as a norm rather than an exception. This behavior is manifested not only in business but in daily life as well. Ghanaian drivers push their way in front of other motorists, regardless of the latter's right of way. In doing so, he compels his fellow motorists to forgo their right of way, allowing the aggressive motorist to have his way in order to avoid accident.

4.4 Leadership and the Creation of a Customer Service Culture

Narver and Slater (1998) identify two dominant approaches used by businesses to create market oriented culture. The first is labelled the *programmatic* approach. This is a *priori* approach in which a business uses education programmes and organisational changes to attempt to implant the desired norms of continuously creating superior value for customers. A second approach is the *market-backed* approach. This is an experiential approach in which a business continuously learns from its day-to-day efforts to create and maintain superior value for customers and, therefore, continuously develops and adapts skills, resources and procedures to satisfy its customers. Marketing theory suggests that both approaches contribute to increasing market orientation. It also suggests that when a priori education of the programatic approach is sharply focused on providing a foundation for the experiential learning, the combined effect of the two learning strategies is the largest.

We suggest that you should work with your colleagues to design an approach that fits the specific needs of your company, drawing inspiration from these perspectives. The first step in developing an effective service delivery system is to recruit people with service mindset – i.e. those with a flair for working and relating with other

Chapter Four | John Kuada & Robert Hinson
Service Marketing in Ghana
London & Abuja, Adonis & Abbey Publishers and
Center for Sustainability and Enterprise Development (CSED)

51

people – for frontline positions. The second step is to provide these people with supportive leadership.

One of the prominent theories of leadership in the management literature is the path-goal theory that explains the relationships between the leader's style and the characteristics of the subordinates and work setting. The theory draws a distinction between two broad leadership styles – the task-oriented and relationship-oriented leadership styles. The two styles have been later labeled *transactional* and *transformational* leadership styles respectively. Transactional leadership perspective focuses on exchanges of favours that occur between leaders and followers and a reward or punishment for good or poor performance. In an earlier development of the transactional leadership perspective, Fiedler (1967) argued that leaders motivate their subordinates in the direction of established goals by clarifying the role and task requirements and by dispensing rewards and punishments as appropriate. His arguments take their roots in the *expectancy theory* which holds that an individual employee's motivation to achieve success is a product of the individual's perceived probability of success and the incentive value (reward) of that success. Similarly, his motivation to avoid failure would be a product of perceived probability of failure and the negative incentive value (punishment) of failure. A manager can, therefore, present rewards as *goals* which his subordinates should aim at. He, then, specifies what subordinates should do (i.e. show the *path*) to earn the rewards. Rewards can take the form of increased pay and/or promotion with increased productivity or training being the presented path. This implies that task-centred managers would simply present company policies on pay and promotion to their subordinates with the understanding that employees will take the required steps to earn them, if they are substantial enough in comparison with the efforts that they are expected to make.

The second leadership perspective – transformational leadership – involves binding people around a common purpose through self-

Chapter Four | John Kuada & Robert Hinson
Service Marketing in Ghana
London & Abuja, Adonis & Abbey Publishers and
Center for Sustainability and Enterprise Development (CSED)

52

reinforcing behaviours that followers gain from successfully achieving a task and from a reliance on intrinsic rewards. Following Oke *et al.*, (2009) transformational leaders act as role models and are able to motivate and inspire their followers by identifying new opportunities, providing meaning and challenge, and articulating a strong vision for the future. They are also enthusiastic and optimistic, communicate clear and realistic expectations and demonstrate commitment to shared visions. Subordinates are encouraged by such leaders to share in the organizational vision, seeing deeper purpose in their work and exceeding their own self-interests for the good of the organization. They also consider the needs of others over their own, are consistent, share risks with others, and conduct themselves ethically. Transformational leaders also provide their followers with individualized consideration- i.e. they focus on followers' individual needs for achievement, development, growth and support. Such leaders also engage in coaching and mentoring, create new learning opportunities and value diversity in their followers. For all these reasons, they are admired, respected and trusted by their followers (Nahavandi, 2009).

Research findings suggest that a climate for superior service delivery and a climate for employee well-being are positively correlated. Both the service climate and human resource management experienced by employees in their organization reflect on how customers experience the service. If an employee is happy with his/her conditions of employment, it will impact positively on his/her ability to show the best performance to delight the customer. It is in the light of these considerations that the relevance of the discussions on leadership must be understood. The understanding is that companies that adopt transformational leadership culture are more likely to build successful customer-oriented cultures. This does not necessarily undervalue the importance of the motivational wisdom underlying the transactional leadership forms. Good salaries and working conditions (as goals) are considered by most employees as basic motivational cues that will encourage them to exert themselves

Chapter Four | John Kuada & Robert Hinson
Service Marketing in Ghana
London & Abuja, Adonis & Abbey Publishers and
Center for Sustainability and Enterprise Development (CSED)

53

in the service of customers. However, in many Ghanaian service companies (e.g. hotels, restaurants and shops), the frontline personnel are the least paid, have the lowest job security and very little training. Some companies even prefer to use casual or temporal employees as front desk staff and telephone exchange operators. Such employees do not enjoy benefits such as medical care that regular staff of the firm enjoys so their level of loyalty and commitment to the companies are low.

Another important issue is that of labour turn-over. This is high in service jobs due to low remuneration, lack of prospects for career advancement, and low job security. An experienced employee is an important asset in a service company due to his or her rich source of tacit knowledge about how customers should be handled. Furthermore, it costs more for an organisation to recruit and train new staff than to motivate and retain experienced staff. It takes a long time to train service personnel to the level at which they can deliver good customer service. It does not make sense to let them go easily only to recruit other people, train them and lose those employees when they are most needed.

Bear in mind, however, that tensions between customers and employees are not entirely avoidable. Disagreements may occur when customers request for services that violate the organizations rules or when a customer makes excessive demands. In such situations, the frontline personnel will often be faced with a hard decision of pleasing the organization or the customer who is supposed to be always right. A transformational leader will create avenues for such employees to vent their frustrations backstage and re-energize themselves in order to serve other customers with smiles.

However, eempirical studies on Ghanaian leadership styles indicate that there is a preponderance of transactional leadership styles in Ghanaian organizations. This makes most employees extremely hesitant to take actions on their own to provide good services to customers. For example, Kuada (1994) showed that

Chapter Four | John Kuada & Robert Hinson
Service Marketing in Ghana
London & Abuja, Adonis & Abbey Publishers and
Center for Sustainability and Enterprise Development (CSED)

54

employees in Ghana tend to act with extreme caution while at work in order not to invite the anger of their superiors for any mistakes that they may make in the course of their work. In his opinion, most African managers hold the view that the principal function of the loyal subordinate in Africa is to serve as a buffer for the immediate superior. If anything goes wrong, the loyal subordinate must do anything to blame all others, including himself, in order to protect his boss. A variation of this kind of behavior plays up in situations where several employees are aware of something that is a problem of mutual concern but they choose to act as if they do not know of it and, therefore, cover up the errors. Argyris (1990) coins the term "skilled incompetence" to describe this type of defensive behavior. The consequence is that employees become very reluctant to question existing practices in their organizations even if this would help rectify operational inefficiencies.

4.5 Summary and Action Points

We have argued earlier that it is good to treat your employees in the same manner as you will treat your customers. When things go wrong, it is the frontline employee that fixes it or refuses to do so. If you have not done so already, you may seriously consider employee job satisfaction as a key factor in your customer-oriented strategy design. When the causes of employee stress are not effectively addressed, they may result in employee frustration and ultimately high employee turnover.

Empower your frontline employees to be willing to take actions that will satisfy customers on the spot. No two customers are the same. Thus, employees should cultivate the mind-set that enables them to vary their approaches to serving people. Your company must also exhibit agility. If one approach does not work for you, if it brings repeated failure, then try something else. But you must develop rules and routines that reduce employees' anxieties about what to do in given situations. It is this combination of empowerment and

Chapter Four | John Kuada & Robert Hinson
Service Marketing in Ghana
London & Abuja, Adonis & Abbey Publishers and
Center for Sustainability and Enterprise Development (CSED)

guidelines that produce dynamic service delivery process in successful service companies.

Chapter Four | John Kuada & Robert Hinson
Service Marketing in Ghana
London & Abuja, Adonis & Abbey Publishers and
Center for Sustainability and Enterprise Development (CSED)

CHAPTER FIVE

Knowing, Assessing and Managing Your Customers

5.1 Introduction

In present day's highly vulnerable and rapidly changing business environment, where survival and success are challenging, every organization needs to adopt the right blend of strategies to attract, retain and maintain customers. Thus, one of your primary functions as a marketing manager is that you must help your company in deciding on which customers you want to target, how you will serve the targeted customers, and how you will differentiate and position your company in the marketplace. This means your company must ask itself the following questions: What values have we provided our customers in their previous encounters with us? Are they sufficient to retain the customers? What kind of services are we going to add to give maximum satisfaction to customers?

These observations reinforce the earlier points we have made that customer knowledge is a key prerequisite in any successful market-oriented strategy implementation. Knowledge is required not only for identifying customer needs and expectations. It is also required to assess the value of each customer to the company over the customer's life time and to retain those customers that promise to make significant contribution to the company's earnings and profit. This chapter is, therefore, devoted to customer knowledge management. It introduces you to some conventional theories and models of how to identify customer needs, how to assess their values and how to ensure their loyalty to your company.

Chapter Five | John Kuada & Robert Hinson
Service Marketing in Ghana
London & Abuja, Adonis & Abbey Publishers and
Center for Sustainability and Enterprise Development (CSED)

5.2 Analysis of New Market Opportunities

Mmanagement must continuously look for new markets whose needs might be met by its current services or slight modifications thereof and at the same time formulate strategies aimed at retaining existing customers. This is what market intelligence systems try to accomplish. A key consideration in new market opportunity assessment is the estimation of the size of demand. Market demand measurement calls for a clear understanding of the market involved.

Various classificatory models have been presented in marketing textbooks to help analysts in gaining insights into the nature of the markets of interest to them. Analysts are usually advised to start their demand measurement with an assessment of the potential market for their products in a given country or industry. The potential market for a product or service is the set of customers who have shown some level of interest in the product. This is different from the available market, which is the set of customers who not only have the need for the product or service but also the income to acquire it.

A distinction is also drawn between the *served* or *target market* and the *penetrated market*. The label "served market" is used to describe that part of the available market that the company is interested in serving and the penetrated market is the set of buyers/ users who have already bought the product. Service providers can, therefore, only target the "un-penetrated" part of the target market or encourage the "penetrated" segment to switch over to their products/services when they are making a repurchase decision.

Toyne and Walter (1989) suggest that a market can be grouped into the following three categories:

- Incipient demand
- latent demand
- Current demand.

Chapter Five | John Kuada & Robert Hinson
Service Marketing in Ghana
London & Abuja, Adonis & Abbey Publishers and
Center for Sustainability and Enterprise Development (CSED)

Incipient market demand: is demand that is expected to exist in the future. For example, if the companies in a specific country are aware of a particular need or want, but lack the resources to acquire the relevant inputs, their needs then constitute incipient market demand. Thus, incipient demand forms part of the potential market for a service provider's product at any given point in time.

Latent market demand: represents an untapped demand. This is the case where a demand exists for a particular product or service, but no company has discovered it and therefore has not offered the customers the desired products or services.

Existing market demand: is what customers in a given country are prepared to pay for. It is the immediately available market for the product. It can be higher than the level of current purchases, since it includes that proportion of demand not as yet satisfied by currently available products due to imperfections in the marketing system.

You must continuously assess all three categories of demand in your analysis of market potentials. While you serve the current customer demand with your portfolio of services, you must also think about what you can do with minimum cost in order to serve latent and incipient demand in the future.

5.3 Understanding Customers and their Behaviour

It is important for your company to invest resources (money and time) to maintain an on-going, healthy, and profitable relationship with your existing customers. To do so, the customers must perceive the relationship as value-adding. In order to help create that value, you must realize that customers are unique and must be treated differently. Consumer behaviour research has shown that understanding any given consumer is not an easy task. Factors that influence consumer decision making include consumers' personality, perception, and their attitude to risk. Some consumers are generally variety-seeking and are not likely to show loyalty to any given service

Chapter Five | John Kuada & Robert Hinson
Service Marketing in Ghana
London & Abuja, Adonis & Abbey Publishers and
Center for Sustainability and Enterprise Development (CSED)

59

provider. Some are impulse buyers. Some consumers are also more motivated to shop for the best prices, while others are more convenience oriented. The multiplicity of behavioural determinants suggests that it will be in your company's interest to use some classificatory models to put your customers into fairly homogenous groups. This will help you to design cost-effective marketing strategies to reach your target customers. The marketing literature refers to this as target marketing.

5.4 Customer Value Analysis

Customer Value Analysis (CVA) is based on the concept of customer-oriented marketing introduced in chapter 3. Basically, customers choose between suppliers by evaluating which supplier provides them with the best *value*. You may start your customer value analysis (CVA) with internal sources of data, drawing on existing information that you already possess about each major customer- sales volume, profits generated, growth trends etc. You may also conduct sample surveys of your company's customers and of its competitors' customers to determine the relative performance of your company on many value attributes. The CVA proceeds along the following steps:

1. Create a profit profile comparing the profit contribution of each customer.
2. Determine the source of the profit
3. Assess the value elements beyond profits – i.e. the relational value of each customer.
4. Determine the overall value ranking within the customer group
5. Determine the marketing requirements for serving the customers
6. Develop a sales/marketing programme commensurate with the customer's value

Chapter Five | John Kuada & Robert Hinson
Service Marketing in Ghana
London & Abuja, Adonis & Abbey Publishers and
Center for Sustainability and Enterprise Development (CSED)

The first three steps allow you to assess the total value of each of your customers. An assessment of the profit contributions of existing customers involves determining sales and profits by each type of service that the customer buys from you. For example, if you are in banking business you may assess the customer's worth in terms of the range of financial services that you provide the customer – pension savings, insurance services, car loans, mortgage loans etc. The profit analysis requires detailed breakdown of marketing costs assignable to the services sold to the customer, including order processing costs and field service costs. Customers are then ranked in terms of profitability.

Figure 5.1 provides an illustration of the dimensions and considerations that go into customer value analysis. The main dimensions in this analysis are the market-perceived quality profile and the market-perceived price profile. These dimensions provide an indication of how much worse or better your company is doing within the target market.

Figure 5.1: A Framework for Customer Value Analysis

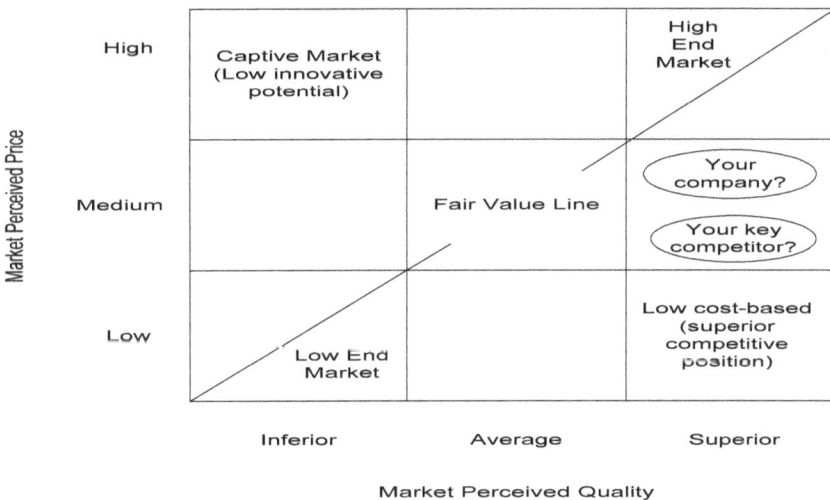

Source: Kuada (2008) pp. 77

Chapter Five | John Kuada & Robert Hinson
Service Marketing in Ghana
London & Abuja, Adonis & Abbey Publishers and
Center for Sustainability and Enterprise Development (CSED)

Share of Purchase Analysis

Pay attention to significant changes in your customers' demand for your services. You can do this by undertaking "share of purchase" (share of wallet) analysis which provides an indication of changes in the customers' purchases. Distinction is usually drawn between present and future sales gap. The present sales gap is the difference between actual sales of the customer of a given service and customers' total purchase volume of service. Thus, if your company provides supplies of only 30% of the total purchases made by the customer of your services, the sales gap is 70%. Your strategy must aim at closing the gap.

You may consider employing key account managers and thus assigning them the task of nursing specific customers. They will be the customers' contact persons in your company. You will find this strategy useful if your company serves several big businesses or organizations. Hence the individual big customer will have one contact person in the company who is in charge of all interaction with and to the specific company. This solution can be far more clear and manageable for both parties. When the same key accounts manager deals with the same group of customers, the risk of communicative misunderstandings are likely to decrease. In this way, the rate of customer complaints will hopefully diminish and the retention of customers increases.

5.5 Customer Retention and Loyalty

Customer retention has been found to be a key factor in improved business performance of most companies. Research has shown that acquiring new customers can cost five times more than the cost involved in satisfying and retaining current customers. The following are some of the reasons:

1. It requires a great deal of effort to induce satisfied customers to switch away from their current suppliers. Therefore, your

Chapter Five | John Kuada & Robert Hinson
Service Marketing in Ghana
London & Abuja, Adonis & Abbey Publishers and
Center for Sustainability and Enterprise Development (CSED)

62

company will save cost if you retain your customers than poach new ones.

2. A highly satisfied customer is most likely to increase the amount of money he or she spends on your company rather than spread his/her purchasing over a host of other service providers.

3. A highly satisfied customer would be prepared to pay a premium price for services rendered if he or she believes to be getting value for money.

4. When highly satisfied customers talk favourably about your company, they become foot soldiers for the company in promoting its services free of charge.

Building on this understanding, your customer value analysis can be further improved by classifying your existing customers in terms of profitability and loyalty. This creates a classificatory matrix of four cells as shown in Figure 5. 2. You may label the various groups of customers as "strangers", "butterflies", "true friends", and "barnacles" depending on their degree of loyalty and profitability. "Strangers" show low potential profitability and little projected loyalty. It is not economically advisable to invest resources in this group of customers. "Butterflies" are potentially profitable but not loyal. You may use promotional blitzes to attract them, create satisfying and profitable transactions with them while they are willing to do business with you. When their interest in your offerings begins to fade, you may cease investing in them until you believe you can capture their attention and interest again. "True friends" are both profitable and loyal. There is a strong fit between their needs and your offerings. You need to make continuous relationship investments to delight, retain and grow them. "Barnacles" are highly loyal but not very profitable. There is a limited fit between their needs and what you are capable of offering them. You may use them as your company's ambassadors.

Chapter Five | John Kuada & Robert Hinson
Service Marketing in Ghana
London & Abuja, Adonis & Abbey Publishers and
Center for Sustainability and Enterprise Development (CSED)

63

Figure 5.2: Customer Loyalty-Profitability Matrix

	High	Butterflies	True Friends
Profitability			
	Low	Strangers	Barnacles
		Low	High

Loyalty

5.5 Summary and Action Points

This chapter provides you with arguments as to why you should design deliberate strategies to retain your customers. Retained customers become loyal customers. You need to develop a simple in-house system of analysis that can provide you with information about the most valuable customers for your company today and tomorrow. This involves three steps:

1. Identify the value-adding customers
2. Targeting the identified customers
3. Serving them better than your competitors

Your company's marketing strategy should outline which customers your company will serve and how it will create value for these customers. You must then develop an integrated marketing programme that will actually deliver the intended value to the customers.

Chapter Five | John Kuada & Robert Hinson
Service Marketing in Ghana
London & Abuja, Adonis & Abbey Publishers and
Center for Sustainability and Enterprise Development (CSED)

CHAPTER SIX

Service Marketing Strategies

6.1 Introduction

We have repeatedly argued that people (employees and customers) must be at the centre stage of all service marketing strategy formulations. We have also argued that although services are generally characterized as being intangible, physical evidence constitutes a key indicator in customers' service expectations and service quality assessments. We said also that you must be mindful of the promises that you make to your potential customers. Your promises shape their service expectations. Finally, we have suggested that the service delivery process itself is essential in any effective customer service management.

This chapter provides you with an overview of marketing tools that you may employ in communicating and delivering the values you have promised your customers. It starts with an introduction to the marketing mix tools.

6.2 Marketing Mix Tools

The most popular set of strategic tools in marketing is the list of marketing variables that have been suggested by Jerome McCarthy – i.e. the 4 Ps. They stand for Product, Price, Promotion and Place.

Product refers to the goods and services you offer to your customers. Apart from the physical product itself, there are elements associated with your product that customers may be attracted to, such as the way it is packaged. Other product attributes include quality, features, options, services, warranties, and brand name. Thus, you might think of what you offer as a bundle of goods and services. Your

Chapter Six | John Kuada & Robert Hinson
Service Marketing in Ghana
London & Abuja, Adonis & Abbey Publishers and
Center for Sustainability and Enterprise Development (CSED)

65

product's appearance, function, and support make up what the customer is actually buying.

Price refers to how much you charge for your product or service. Determining your product's price can be tricky and even frightening. Very low prices may be perceived by customers as a signal of low quality. You must decide on a price that adequately reflects value and give you a reasonable profit. Remember that price increases represent a potential threat to the establishment and maintenance of long-term customer relationships and loyalty. Price increases are sometimes unavoidable, for example, when input costs rise. According to the literature, longer term customers should be less price-sensitive. This is another reason why customer retention strategies are useful.

Promotion refers to the advertising and selling part of marketing. It is how you let people know what you've got for sale. The purpose of promotion is to get people to understand what your product or service is what they can use it for, and why they should want it.

Place refers to the distribution channels used to get your product to your customers. But the distribution avenues for services are constrained by the fact that they cannot be stored and transported.

Over time, many academic commentators came to consider the 4Ps as woefully incomplete and inadequate for marketing strategy formulation. Others have suggested additional "Ps". Boom and Bitner in 1981 added three more Ps - people, physical environment and processes to make it appropriate for service marketing. These have become known as the 7Ps of the services marketing mix.

People in this context include all people involved either directly or indirectly in the consumption of a service. Physical evidence covers the way that service is delivered and needs to be communicated and followed through. Since you are creating an intangible experience, communication and documentation is the only physical evidence you have to share with your consumer. Make sure you are doing enough of it. Process for him means procedures and flow of activities of how services are consumed.

Chapter Six | John Kuada & Robert Hinson
Service Marketing in Ghana
London & Abuja, Adonis & Abbey Publishers and
Center for Sustainability and Enterprise Development (CSED)

The latest development in the marketing mix discussion comes from Kotler and Keller (2012) who have proposed the following 4Ps to replace those suggested by McCarthy: People, Process, Programme and Performance. We have repeatedly argued that all people directly or indirectly involved in the consumption of a service are an important part of the extended marketing mix. "People" in Kotler and Keller's 4Ps, therefore, refer to all actors involved in the marketing process. They include employees, consumers, regulatory and facilitative institutions and the civil society. "Processes" refer to procedures, mechanisms and the flow of activities by which services are consumed (customer management processes). They also include innovative efforts, creativity and discipline in the marketing management process. Programmes in this context are the old 4Ps which Kotler and Keller still consider essential for effective marketing efforts. Performance: covers both economic and non-economic performance indicators (profits, growth, market share and social as well as environmental benefits of marketing efforts).

6.3 Marketing Communication Mix

There is a growing awareness among service providers that marketing communication tools are highly important in the overall effectiveness of their service marketing strategies. The marketing literature presents the marketing communications mix as the specific mix of advertising, personal selling, sales promotion, public relations, and direct marketing that your company may use to achieve its marketing objectives. Advertising is, therefore, seen as a powerful communication tool in marketing. It is defined as any paid form of non-personal presentation and promotion of ideas, goods, or services by an identified sponsor. Personal selling is a personal presentation of your services by your sales people for the purpose of encouraging them to buy your services. It also helps to build customer relationships. Sales promotions represent short-term incentives to encourage the purchase of your services. Public relations are all activities that your company may undertake to build a good corporate image.

Companies communicate certain promises to potential consumers

Chapter Six | John Kuada & Robert Hinson
Service Marketing in Ghana
London & Abuja, Adonis & Abbey Publishers and
Center for Sustainability and Enterprise Development (CSED)

67

through their promotional strategies. There are explicit promises that service providers communicate to potential customers. These can be personal and non-personal statements. The statements are personal when they are communicated by sales people or service/repair personnel. They are non-personal when they come from advertising, brochures and other written publications. These promises raise the expectations of customers to the extent that they influence both the levels of desired service and predicted service.

One main objective of professional service communication is to give assurance and to reduce uncertainty in the minds of potential clients who are yet to experience the service of the firm. Potential consumers of the service need assurance that service providers would deliver quality and satisfactory services.

There are also implicit service promises. These are service-related cues rather than explicit promises that lead to inferences about what the service should and will be like. These inferences may be derived from the price and tangibles associated with the service. For example, the higher rates charged at a five star hotel like the Sheraton in Abuja as well as the serene impressive surroundings suggest the provision of a higher quality than from a two star African hotel with lower rates and less impressive facilities.

When deciding how to properly utilize the marketing communications mix to meet your marketing objectives, it is important to consider the relative strengths and weaknesses of each component of the mix. You will balance the various parts of the mix to not only create an integrated approach to your marketing communications but you must also devote enough resources for each component to be successful.

Your company must examine a wide range of communication tools before deciding on which of them will serve the company's interests best. Some of the tools are described in details below

Chapter Six | John Kuada & Robert Hinson
Service Marketing in Ghana
London & Abuja, Adonis & Abbey Publishers and
Center for Sustainability and Enterprise Development (CSED)

Visual Pathways to Quality

Visual pathways refer to all the printed materials of your company. These include, brochures, which showcase company profiles, detailing all the information on the company, capabilities, professional qualifications and experiences. Make sure that they provide you with a good image. These visuals also serve as a measure of pre-service experience quality. Consumers can develop their service expectations and perceptions based on the company's printed material carried in their communications.

Letters

Sales letters are basically written to persuade the reader to buy a product or service, support a cause, or participate in an activity. It is also meant to introduce a product or service to potential customers. Each sales letter follows what is called the **"four A's"**. It should get the readers' ATTENTION, highlight the product's APPEAL, and show the customers the product's. APPLICATION, and end with a specific request for ACTION.

It is particularly important to call attention to the service's appeal. Once the customer's attention has been aroused, all the service attributes should always be carefully articulated to the customer. The last part of the letter should elicit action from the customer. The purpose of a sales letter is missed if the customer ignores your request for action. The customer should come to some purchase decision and in the case of non-purchase; the customer's reasons should be solicited for future action.

Talk to your reader directly in your letters. This means you must avoid using first person pronouns such as 'I', 'We' and 'My'. An effort should be made to concentrate rather on the use of the word 'You'. For example, write 'Your requested data is enclosed' or 'your invoice will be ready on Monday'. You must also avoid the use of negative phrases and respond positively to requests. For example, you should

Chapter Six | John Kuada & Robert Hinson
Service Marketing in Ghana
London & Abuja, Adonis & Abbey Publishers and
Center for Sustainability and Enterprise Development (CSED)

write; 'Please call with your passport sized photograph', rather than, 'You failed to come along with your passport sized photograph'. Reminding your employees to respond to requests should be done with courtesy and appreciation.

Telephone Etiquette

The first contact a prospective customer is likely to make with your company is by telephone. The way the telephone is answered can tell the whole story about the kind of service customers can expect to receive from you. The correct phrases said in the right order can give a positive first impression and convey an immediate message about your company. Almost the entire message projected to the customer over the telephone is communicated through the tone of the voice; so it does not take long for the customer to pick up the attitude.

The following can be done to improve the quality of your telephone conversations with customers:

- Smile when talking on the phone
- Practice stressing words
- Breath deep, long and slow
- Make deliberate efforts to sound and feel friendly
- Show willingness to help and answer the telephone by the third ring.
- Use a voice tone that conveys sincerity and gives undivided attention.
- Speak clearly, use correct grammar and use descriptive words.
- Do not use first names.
- Return calls promptly.

If a customer is angry and speaking loudly, one does not have to yell back, even though the instinctive reaction may be to do so. Instead, behave like a professional and start out by speaking somewhat at a lower volume than the customer, gradually bringing the customer's volume down to your level. With a confused customer,

Chapter Six | John Kuada & Robert Hinson
Service Marketing in Ghana
London & Abuja, Adonis & Abbey Publishers and
Center for Sustainability and Enterprise Development (CSED)

speaking a little louder than usual helps give him or her something to focus on and helps you to control the conversation more easily.

6.4 Online Marketing Tools

The advent of the Internet has provided marketing managers with a new set of powerful marketing communication tools. These include emails, viral marketing possibilities and new methods of advertising. We will discuss some of the opportunities presented by the internet briefly under this section.

E-mail

E-mail or electronic mail has become a popular way of communicating. It is quick, barring any heavy network traffic. It is convenient and can be delivered even if the receiver is away from his computer. It is also cost-effective and cheaper than making multiple telephone calls. Sending and receiving e-mails make conducting business easier than using the conventional channels.

An e-mail ought to follow a certain format. It is unadvisable to send messages all written in capital letters or in lower case letters. It is just like shouting at your readers. It makes reading difficult and if one receiver decides to make a hard copy, it will be a clear departure from a professional correspondence.

It is professional to include a return mail address including a telephone number and title of your message. It saves the receiver the trouble of looking it up. Use clear, specific and complete descriptions for your subject line. For example, if it is on an unpaid account, it is prudent to have a subject line that accurately reflects this.

It is also important to respect your e-mail audience and observe the internet etiquette. State your reason for the e-mail in the first line. This catches the attention of the reader. Do not send an unsolicited e-mail without prior verification whether your targets want to receive it.

Chapter Six | John Kuada & Robert Hinson
Service Marketing in Ghana
London & Abuja, Adonis & Abbey Publishers and
Center for Sustainability and Enterprise Development (CSED)

Remember that an e-mail is not entirely private and several firms monitor the e-mails of their employees. Avoid sarcasm and humour and do not use emoticons in business writing. You must also keep in mind that the receiver of your e-mail will be reading it on a computer and not on a piece of paper. Therefore, keep your message succinct and to the point.

The task is to make the mail relevant and at the right time. A thorough programme of triggered messages (sent individually based on website behaviour) can provide tremendous information about a subscriber while simultaneously delivering hyper-relevant and timely information. This means that companies contemplating the use of email marketing must analyse visitors to websites in order to know when to send a specific message to a particular visitor.

Viral Marketing

Viral marketing is word of mouth translated into internet marketing, and can be seen as the herd-behaviour in social relations. Many people have a tradition for passing funny emails on, or having a specific Friday ritual of wishing good weekend with a joke. This social relational phenomenon has now become part of a marketing tool, whereby ambassadors of products create advertising by highlighting their experiences with products or service. In this way, viral marketing has become cheaper than normal advertising option since the advertiser, in theory, only has to post the advertisement in one place, and let it spread from there. Furthermore, viral marketing is often not even perceived as commercial advertising, as the person behind the message often is a friend or co-worker. Viral marketing often has the possibility to reach consumers that a company normally would not reach with any advertising option. Many companies today are very much aware of viral marketing, and typically have their advertising material available online and allow for such materials to be sent to friends.

Chapter Six | John Kuada & Robert Hinson
Service Marketing in Ghana
London & Abuja, Adonis & Abbey Publishers and
Center for Sustainability and Enterprise Development (CSED)

Banner Ads

One of the most widely used forms of advertising online is that of the banner ad. The ad is placed on a website, and usually highlights itself with different colours, sizes and motions. It can be a punch line, a question or even a video. It has evolved with the discovery of newer tools and programmes. In the beginning, the banner was a non-moving square with a text and/or picture, but today it is often a video that starts with a mouse over. Therefore, the banner ad can be compared to an outdoor communication form that developed with the internet.

Recently, several researchers have shown that banner ads also have an impact on consumers' attitude towards a brand independent of click-through rate. It was shown that banner ads have longer-term effects that help build brand equity and can successfully raise brand awareness, preference, and consumer purchase intentions.

6.5 Strategies for Effective Customer Visits

The image that customers create in their minds' eye during their first encounter with you is critical to their final decision to select your company as a service provider. It influences the perception that they carry about the service, the people, the environment, speed, responsibility, responsiveness and all other factors that are used to evaluate the service experience, and those that have a bearing on the total service quality. A customer, who visits a bank for the first time and is delighted, would carry that impression and it would be difficult for any other person to convince him to change his perception about the quality of service in that bank. Similarly, a customer who carries away the impression that the service personnel of the bank are rude and irresponsible would be difficult to convince to change his perception.

First impressions also create what is called the 'hallo effect' during the service encounter. Once customers form their impression

Chapter Six | John Kuada & Robert Hinson
Service Marketing in Ghana
London & Abuja, Adonis & Abbey Publishers and
Center for Sustainability and Enterprise Development (CSED)

73

within the first few minutes, this impression is likely to influence the rest of the proceedings during the encounter. Take for example, a customer who visits the booking office of an airline. The reception area is exquisite with flowers; a senior officer meets him and takes the customer through the process before taking him/her to the officer in charge. The initial impression is likely to influence all other decisions that would be taken. On the other hand, if the customer has a confrontation with a very rude security person before entering the office, he /she may end up not buying or making certain decisions because of the first impression of an unprofessional encounter.

6.6 Summary and Action Points

Marketing strategy may be defined as a set of specific ideas and actions that outline and guide decisions on the best or chosen way to create, distribute, promote, and price a product or service (manage the marketing mix variables). The most popular marketing mix variables are classified as 4Ps. Effective marketing mix strategies must fulfil the following 4 requirements:

1. Match customer needs
2. Create competitive advantage
3. Match corporate resources
4. Blend the various dimensions well

It must be noted that all the efforts and investments that your company makes in order to attract customers will come to naught, if there is a negative first impression during a service encounter. It is, therefore, important for you to have a systematic means of developing people and service ambience to take advantage of first impressions. You must also train your front line staff such as security personnel and front office executives to be knowledgeable and courteous in dealing with potential customers.

Chapter Six | John Kuada & Robert Hinson
Service Marketing in Ghana
London & Abuja, Adonis & Abbey Publishers and
Center for Sustainability and Enterprise Development (CSED)

CHAPTER SEVEN

Managing Customer Complaints

7.1 Introduction

You must expect occasional mistakes in your service delivery process, no matter how well your employees try. A customer may accidentally be overcharged for service, there may be power outage, your inputs supplier may disappoint you or a frontline employee may have a bad day. Customer complaint is, therefore, not entirely avoidable. Your responsibility as a service provider is to respond to the customer's complaints in a manner that increases satisfaction. Even though complaints may sometimes seem undesirable, they nevertheless serve as a source of important feedback for your company. They contain the direct voice of the customer. If complaints are transformed into knowledge about customers, they can provide a valuable amount of goodwill for your company. A bank teller for example, has no business snapping at a customer if the customer complains about the long wait he has had to endure before he got served. The customer's complaint is a free message to the bank that service might be too slow and customers may be uncomfortable about it. Complaining customers could be the most loyal customers of your company, if their complaints are well handled. Your company must, therefore, design, build, operate and continuously upgrade systems for managing complaints. These systems are called customer complaint management systems (CCMS).

This chapter aims at improving your understanding of why customers complain and what you can do to handle these complains effectively and turns them into opportunities to strengthen your relationships with your key customers.

Chapter Seven | John Kuada & Robert Hinson
Service Marketing in Ghana
London & Abuja, Adonis & Abbey Publishers and
Center for Sustainability and Enterprise Development (CSED)

7.2 The Value of Customer Complaints

Service marketing scholars have observed that complaints are potentially useful to a company if properly handled. They provide an opportunity to discover weaknesses in service provisions; identify areas for improvement and demonstrate high levels of customer care in resolving issues. Furthermore, effective customer complaint procedures can help organizations to improve service quality by offering unhappy customers a channel through which they can make their voices heard by their service providers. Thus, information from complainants provides free feedback on service provision and results in one of the best forms of free market research for a company.

Zairi (2000) identifies 6 benefits that customer complaints may offer a service company. These are:

1. They are a way of receiving feedback from customers and therefore a necessary means for putting into action, improvement plans.
2. They are a tool for preventing complacency and harnessing internal competencies for optimizing service delivery systems.
3. They are a useful way of measuring performance and allocating resources to deal with the deficient areas of the service business.
4. They are a useful "mirror" for gauging internal performance against competition.
5. They are a useful exercise for getting nearer customers and understanding them better.
6. Complaining customers are among the most loyal customers, if their complaints are satisfactorily handled.

Despite these advantages, your company may find customer complaints highly irritating for the following reasons:

1. If you lack a systematic approach to complaints   handling.

Chapter Seven | John Kuada & Robert Hinson
Service Marketing in Ghana
London & Abuja, Adonis & Abbey Publishers and
Center for Sustainability and Enterprise Development (CSED)

76

2. If you do not recognize the importance of customer complaints at a strategic level.

3. If you do not train your employees to respond positively to complaints

4. If you have allowed the development of "blame and reprimand" culture in your company.

5. If you have not embraced the concept of quality management and its related concepts.

7.3 Reasons why your Customers Complain

Since complaints arise from customer dissatisfaction with services, it is important to first examine the reasons for customer dissatisfaction and complaints in Ghana before examining the reasons for poor handling of customer complaints by organizations. From our experience and interactions with consumers, customer dissatisfaction and poor service provision in our society arises from the following:

Failure of Service Providers to Meet Customers' Expectation

This is mainly due to the fact that most service providers raise the expectations of customers above what they can provide. An example is occurrences in the real estate industry in Ghana, where there have been complaints from customers because the brochures and other advertising materials give the customers an expectation of what their finished houses would look like. The actual houses delivered frequently turn out to be different from customers' expectation.

Failure of Service Providers to Inform Customers of Probable Inability to Fulfil Promises

In a developing country like Ghana, many factors militate against the ability of service providers to fulfil promises. For example, unexpected traffic situations and unnecessary bureaucracy can prevent a service provider from adhering to time schedules. Whatever

Chapter Seven | John Kuada & Robert Hinson
Service Marketing in Ghana
London & Abuja, Adonis & Abbey Publishers and
Center for Sustainability and Enterprise Development (CSED)

77

the reason for the inability to perform, you must quickly inform the customer of the possible inability to meet his or her expectations.

Lack of Adequate Competition

A few years ago the lack of adequate competition caused most Ghanaian service organizations to treat customers poorly and disregard customer complaints. Ghana Telecom previously had a monopoly in telecommunication services. Services were poor and customer satisfaction was not regarded as an important element in the organization's success, until there were new entrants into the industry and the company started losing market share. Ghana Telecom is now struggling to match competition and has become a follower to 'Scancom', the current leader in the mobile phone industry in Ghana. Services rendered by Ghana Broadcasting Corporation were far from satisfactory. At the time, it was the only television station in the country. Though its services are still not up to desirable standards, the proliferation of the television media has caused them to marginally improve the services.

Lack of Good Customer Service Culture

We have argued earlier that service excellence has never been a part of the Ghanaian culture. Most personnel in service organizations have seen themselves as doing a favour to the customer rather than the opposite. Customers themselves have failed to insist on their rights to satisfactory service and resolution of their complaints.

Hinson (2006) distinguishes between two types of dissatisfied customers: the "passives" – i.e. those who do not take action because they believe complaining is not worth the effort and will only cause additional annoyance and waste of time or who instead of telling the provider, tell others and talk to third parties through negative word of mouth, and the "garruls" (garrulous/talkative people) who insist on their right for compensation. These are gradually changing.

Chapter Seven | John Kuada & Robert Hinson
Service Marketing in Ghana
London & Abuja, Adonis & Abbey Publishers and
Center for Sustainability and Enterprise Development (CSED)

Whichever type of customer the complainant is, it is your duty to handle the complaints with the seriousness that you will attend to the complaints of a member of a royal family.

7.4 Approaches to Complaints Management

Effective handling of customer complaints can only be achieved if there is a well-designed customer complaint management system that effectively captures customer complaints and ensures a speedy and satisfactory resolution of the complaints. Ghanaian companies that have complaint handling systems usually capture customer complaints through self-completed questionnaires and the provision of 'suggestion boxes'; soliciting suggestions and opinions from customers.   These measures are, however, not adequate to encourage complaints from customers. Customers themselves feel it is a waste of time writing out complaints and putting them in the boxes. The boxes are seen as more of a public relations tool than a genuine encouragement to receive complaints. There is no assurance that the complaint will be received and attended to. Where the complaint is received, there is normally no feedback from the organization to the customer thanking him or her for making the complaint or suggestion and assuring him or her that the issues raised will be attended to.

Here are some suggestions you may need to consider. First, offer customers the opportunity to contact your company directly and talk to you – possibly on the phone. When they do so, take deliberate steps to respond to your customers' emotional state. It is important to remain calm when listening to a complaint and also to calm the customer when a difficulty arises so that the problem can be solved amicably for the business relationship to be maintained. Allow the customer to vent his/her anger without interrupting. Train your employees in the art of listening and speaking. Employees who attend to customers' complaints should show empathy. They must thank the customer for bringing the problem to their attention and avoid

Chapter Seven | John Kuada & Robert Hinson
Service Marketing in Ghana
London & Abuja, Adonis & Abbey Publishers and
Center for Sustainability and Enterprise Development (CSED)

blaming others or making excuses. They must learn to routinely use some of the following phrases:

'I understand how frustrating this is to you.'
'I'm sorry we let you down.'
'Let's see what we can do to fix the problem.'
'I appreciate how you feel.'
'I don't blame you for being upset.'
'I understand that you have been inconvenienced.'

Second, agree on procedures for handling complaints and train your employees in how to follow the procedures. But it is important to empower your employees to show creativity in finding solutions to the problem on the spot (if possible) or suggest several options and let the customer select. When appropriate, follow up with a telephone call.

Case 7.1

Poor Internal Customer Service at Merchant Bank

Mr. Kingsley Amoateng is the Customer Service Manager in Bibiani branch of the Merchant Bank Ghana Limited (MBG). He joined this bank in 2000 after graduating from the University of Ghana. He started as a Customer Service Officer and got promoted to Customer Service Manager in 2008. Mr. Kingsley Amoateng was nervous about the fall of the market share of the bank. According to the 2013 Banking Survey conducted by accounting professionals, Price Water House Coopers, MBG dropped one place to join the tier of two categories. Mr. Kingsley Amoateng had a reason to worry. He had received an email from the Head Office that the market share of his branch had reduced by 5% in the first quartile in 2014. The email specified that if the market share of his branch did not improve at the end of the year, he would be replaced as Customer Service Manager. Again, he had a second reason to worry because some employees were dissatisfied with responses they received from unit heads in the company to requests they made. To them, the slow internal responses made it difficult for them to render

---

Chapter Seven | John Kuada & Robert Hinson
Service Marketing in Ghana
London & Abuja, Adonis & Abbey Publishers and
Center for Sustainability and Enterprise Development (CSED)

80

satisfactory services to the bank's customers. They registered their grievances with Mr. Kingsley Amoateng who then held a series of meetings with the Customer Service representative and the Tellers of the bank. One of the episodes narrated during these meetings was about a customer who wanted to withdraw an amount of money from the bank. The amount he asked for was above the limit of the teller who was to serve him. The teller then notified the accountant for authorization. She called the accountant after 10 minutes but did not receive response. Tarrying for 30 minutes, the customer became angry and confronted the teller saying that if they were not ready to give him the money, they should let him know. The teller went to the accountant's office but was asked for more time since the accountant was busy. It took about an hour for the accountant to give the authorization irrespective of the pressure the teller gave. In fact, the customer was very unhappy with the situation. The teller was also frustrated and felt demotivated by the episode since she felt that the accountant did not consider her request seriously enough.

Assignment

What lessons can you draw from this case?

7.6 Summary and Action Points

The causes of complaints are many. The following are some of the causes:

- Failure of service providers to meet customers' expectations
- Failure of service providers to inform customers of probable inability to fulfil promises
- Undue bureaucratic delays
- Lack of good customer service skills
- Inexperienced and ill-trained service providers

Improving complaint handling in your company will require taking the following steps:

Chapter Seven | John Kuada & Robert Hinson
Service Marketing in Ghana
London & Abuja, Adonis & Abbey Publishers and
Center for Sustainability and Enterprise Development (CSED)

81

- Managing and training of employees in customer service practices and ability to resolve customer issues and meet the needs and expectations of customers
- Empowering of employees to resolve complaints
- Communication of best practices throughout your company
- Updating system performance measurements

Chapter Seven | John Kuada & Robert Hinson
Service Marketing in Ghana
London & Abuja, Adonis & Abbey Publishers and
Center for Sustainability and Enterprise Development (CSED)

82

CHAPTER EIGHT

Building B2B Marketing Relationships

8.1 Introduction

The concept of relationship marketing (RM) has been described as a new marketing paradigm and a new marketing strategy (Aijo 1996). Companies have become increasingly conscious of the fact that unique (i.e. non-imitable) and superior customer value is best created through relationships. This allows service providers to retain their customers over a longer period of time than they used to. Service providers now see customer retention as a goal in itself.

Kotler (1991) expresses the development in the following words: "What I think we are witnessing today is a movement away from a focus on exchange - in the narrow sense of transaction - and towards a focus on building value-laden relationships and marketing networks. We start thinking mostly about how to hold on to our existing customers.... Our thinking is therefore moving from a marketing mix focus to a relationship focus"[1].

Crucial elements in the RM framework include interactivity, networking, trust, long term orientation and exchange of promises. As Shapiro et al., (1995 p. 186) explain it, "relationship selling is not just a better set of techniques for making sales. It is a different philosophy based upon continuity and trust". Concepts such as symbiotic marketing, co-marketing alliances, internal marketing are now widely used in the literature to explain the characteristics of relationship marketing.

Several factors have contributed to the importance of RM in current business practices. They include the general affluence in the Western industrialised economies, globalisation, technological innovations,

---

[1] Kotler, P. (1991) Marketing Science Review Spring

Chapter Eight | John Kuada & Robert Hinson
Service Marketing in Ghana
London & Abuja, Adonis & Abbey Publishers and
Center for Sustainability and Enterprise Development (CSED)

information revolutions (computer and telecommunication developments) all of which have combined to produce a buyer's market characterised by limitless buyer choices. These circumstances have compelled companies to simultaneously raise efficiency through cost minimisation and improve the level of quality of their products. Quality expectations of customers everywhere have increased. To serve them, service providers must have up-to-date awareness of these expectations and work with them to succeed.

As marketers of consumer products and services come under increasing pressure to be strategically flexible and to mass-customise, they put pressure on their suppliers as well to reduce cost and improve quality. To achieve these twin goals of low cost and high quality of products and delivery services, it has become imperative for firms to collaborate closely in their business-to-business transactions.

Box 8.1

Your relationships with customers will provide you with new ideas, new ways of enhancing the value of your services as well as new ways of communicating these values to your customers.

It is, therefore, important to encourage your employees to make it a habit to talk to new and regular customers. Create time for them to do so.

8.2 Typology of Relationships

Four broad types of service provider-customer relationships can be identified:

1. *Systematic sought out relationship:* is where service providers conduct elaborate market search to identify customers and design proactive marketing strategies aimed at building relationship with them.

Chapter Eight | John Kuada & Robert Hinson
Service Marketing in Ghana
London & Abuja, Adonis & Abbey Publishers and
Center for Sustainability and Enterprise Development (CSED)

84

2. *Emergent relationship is* where initial transactions with customers lead to incremental development of relationship. This happens when customers are satisfied with the outcome of the initial transactions.
3. *Arranged relationships.* They are the types of relationships that are initiated by third parties, e.g. on the initiative of a public institution as part of government policy.
4. *Strategically unavoidable relationships.* These are relationships that companies consider imperative for the sustenance of their competitive advantages. For example, a hotel may outsource its catering services.

Business-to-Business service marketing relationships are most often likened to marriage. Both partners believe that each has unique skills and functional abilities the other lacks. They bring into the relationship a faith that they will be stronger together than either would be separately and they are willing to work diligently over time to make the union work. This is how the hotel and the catering service provider must conceive their relationships.

The process starts with selection and courtship. The service provider first assesses its service offerings and matches them against the expectations of the customer in order to determine its ability to fulfil these expectations. Contacts are then initiated and agreements are worked out and signed. After these details of the relationships are negotiated and implemented. The interactions between the staff of the buyer and service provider lead to the identification of problems, the discovery of differences and the agreement of acceptable approaches to solving emerging problems. At some point in the future exit becomes inevitable, either through "death or divorce". To manage the relationships effectively, it is important for both the service provider and customer organisations to empower their front line personnel to take decisions that can smooth the process of interaction.

Companies engaged in relationship marketing must, therefore, be mindful of the fact that relationships involve a substantial loss of

John Kuada & Robert Hinson
Service Marketing in Ghana
London & Abuja, Adonis & Abbey Publishers and
Center for Sustainability and Enterprise Development (CSED)

autonomy. As Shapiro et al (1995 p. 184) explain it, "decisions will no longer be made only on the basis of the needs and desires of one organisation, but on the joint needs and desires of both partners."

Key Accounts Management

Relationship marketing is resource demanding, in terms of management time and broad management involvement in all aspects of the relationship. In order to manage a service provider's resources effectively, customers may be classified in terms of the sizes of businesses transacted or expected to be transacted with them as well as the amount of resources that they expect to devote to them. Major customers receive high quality of coordinated support from a variety of functional units (e.g. sales, technical support services, and marketing) within the company. The management of such relationships has been dubbed *strategic accounts management* and is based on the following three attributes:

1. Importance
2. Intimacy
3. Longevity

Importance relates to the sales and/or profit that can be generated from a particular account. Customers must be expected to represent high financial pay-outs for service providers to devote substantial resources to them. Intimacy allows service providers and customers to gain insight into each other's businesses, and to share operating information. **Intimacy** is based on trust and trust in turn promotes intimacy. (See the discussion of trust below). **Longevity** of relationships is also necessary to encourage companies to invest the required resources in the relationship in the hope that the partners will reap the anticipated rewards from their investments.

In the very intense relationships, service providers may have to post their employees in the customer's organisation to work together with the customer's employees. In such situations, strong personal

Chapter Eight | John Kuada & Robert Hinson
Service Marketing in Ghana
London & Abuja, Adonis & Abbey Publishers and
Center for Sustainability and Enterprise Development (CSED)

86

relationships may develop between the employees of the two companies and influence the longevity of the relationship. The close collaboration will enable the service provider to gain good knowledge on how its product is used and help develop unique applications for the focal customers. The buyer is also willing to share such knowledge with the service provider as long as this will help him or her to gain new knowledge and unique support for its activities from its service provider company. The knowledge leads to improvements in the competitive positions for both companies.

1. It is important that service providers avoid the following four types of errors in the management of their strategic accounts:
2. Attempting to develop too many strategic account relationships.
3. Picking poor strategic account partners.
4. Allocating too few resources to the relationship.
5. Losing sight of the importance of cultural compatibility in the relationships.

In order to satisfy key accounts fully and explore opportunities that emerge from the relationship, it is essential that the number of accounts must match company resources. Since service providers have to concentrate their resources on few accounts, the selected accounts must be truly strategic in terms of business volume. A poor choice will naturally lead to waste resources and high opportunity cost.

In closing, it must be noted that strategic accounts justify and require the broader involvement of the best managers/employees of the service provider and customer organisations. An inability to assign adequate staff to the relationship or empowering them to make quick decisions can act as a serious constraint to the performance of the relationship. Furthermore, focusing on quick financial performance of such relationship can jeopardise its prospects. This implies that companies entering into the relationship must have some

Chapter Eight | John Kuada & Robert Hinson
Service Marketing in Ghana
London & Abuja, Adonis & Abbey Publishers and
Center for Sustainability and Enterprise Development (CSED)

87

degree of slack resources to start with and may be able to leverage external resources when necessary.

Finally, if personal relationships are to develop, people must spend time together. Improvements in information technology (intra and internet facilities) have added new possibilities for interaction even in the absence of geographical proximity.

8.3 Trust and Business Relationships

Trust is widely recognised as a critical component in successful relationship marketing. In the social science literature, trust is believed to be that social attribute that generates a willingness among people in dyadic relations to sacrifice their short-run individual self-interests for the attainment of joint goals or longer term objectives (Sabel, 1993). People who trust each other believe that their relationships are worth sustaining and, therefore, actively contribute to its continuity. That is, trust leads to higher levels of loyalty and long term collaboration between people (Fukuyama 1995).

Similar perspectives are reflected in the B2B marketing literature. Anderson and Narus (1990 p.45) define trust as "the firm's belief that another firm will perform actions that result in positive outcomes for the firm, as well as not take unexpected actions that would result in negative outcomes for the firm". Trust allows firms to reduce or avoid reliance on costly formal monitoring mechanisms to maintain their partnership. It also produces mutual concern for longer term benefits by partners, raises market performance through the improvement of efficiency, and allows for information exchange, joint problem solving attitude and mutual learning (Aulakh, Kotabe and Sahay, 1996). Furthermore, trust complements written contracts between firms. A contract cannot be expected to address every eventuality and contingency faced over the course of a long-term relationship. Where trust exists between the partners, they will adapt to unanticipated contingencies without resorting to opportunism. As Sabel (1993) observes, trust requires a mutual suspension of self-interest of the

Chapter Eight | John Kuada & Robert Hinson
Service Marketing in Ghana
London & Abuja, Adonis & Abbey Publishers and
Center for Sustainability and Enterprise Development (CSED)

interacting partners. That is, it lays the foundation for a mutual confidence among business partners that no party to an exchange will exploit the other's vulnerability. Universal suspicion is, therefore, replaced by shared confidence.

The need for cultural sensitivity is closely related to trust between cross-national partners. The argument here is that cultural sensitivity promotes regular and effective communication between the collaborating firms and thereby reduces the incidence of misunderstanding and suspicion. Trust is, therefore, seen as a culture-dependent concept. That is, the underlying logics of trust differ across societies. Thus, Johnson *et al* (1996) found a wide discrepancy between Japanese and Western ideas of trust. They further noted that the rules of trust building observed by partners based in the same culture differ from those observed by partners belonging to different cultures.

8.4 Summary and Actions Points

If your company provides services to other companies and organizations, you must pay extra attention to building and managing your relationships with your customers. This is because the cost of losing a single customer may create havoc for you. These are some of the actions you may need to take:

1. Does a customer value analysis for each of your customers?
2. Assign each customer to a key account manager.
3. Encourage regular interactions between your key account managers and your customers.
4. Be informed about possible complaints and how they have been addressed.
5. Undertake periodic visits to your customers in order to symbolically demonstrate how important they are to your company.

Chapter Eight | John Kuada & Robert Hinson
Service Marketing in Ghana
London & Abuja, Adonis & Abbey Publishers and
Center for Sustainability and Enterprise Development (CSED)

CHAPTER NINE

Marketing and Professional Service Providers

9.1 Introduction

We have argued that the most successful businesses are those that recognize the value of their customer base and exploit that value most effectively. Such organizations put in just as much (or perhaps even more) effort into retaining existing customers as they put into attracting new ones. We have also argued that customers tend to learn more about quality from others since that is seen to be more credible than company sources. Thus, once a service company gains a positive reputation through improved quality, it becomes very easy for existing customers to make referrals to prospective new customers. Companies and industries that have been operating within a competitive service sector for several years are aware of these issues. But this is not true for many professional service providers including architects, lawyers and accounting firms. They are relative newcomers to the field of marketing and have limited competencies in marketing their own services and in buying services from each other. Not in the very distant past, many of these firms tended to adopt "may-the-best-man-win" position when bidding for an assignment. They are reluctant to promote their services or market their firms in any visible way.

If you are a manager in one of such companies or if your company serves firms in any of these industries the present chapter brings together most of the ideas presented earlier in this book in order to provide you a synthesis that will guide your marketing strategy formulation and implementation. It will provide you with some understanding of the importance of marketing for your company and give you some guidelines for designing an effective marketing strategy.

Chapter Nine | John Kuada & Robert Hinson
Service Marketing in Ghana
London & Abuja, Adonis & Abbey Publishers and
Center for Sustainability and Enterprise Development (CSED)

9.2 Characteristics of Professional Services

Professional services refer to the delivery of intangible offerings such as physician services, architectural services, legal services, accounting services and management services. Professional service companies have relatively fewer transactions. For example, a lawyer may have only a few firms or individual clients with specific needs and requirement for the firm to handle. This makes their marketing and communication processes quite challenging in comparison to other service companies.

It is important to remember that no two clients of a professional service provider are alike. Even patients with similar symptoms may be radically different from each other due to their biological compositions. Therefore, professional services are process oriented, - i.e. The production process needs to be carefully managed in order to ensure a successful service encounter. For example, the pre-consumption evaluation would depend on the image of the service firm, word of mouth from satisfied customers and other communications from the firm. A hotel customer has the opportunity to examine the facilities in the hotel before deciding to make a reservation. On the other hand, it is relatively difficult for a client of a management consultant to do so.

In management consulting, the consultant needs to develop a systematic approach to analyse the firm's problems in order to derive a strategy for implementation. Similarly, a lawyer would need to study the relevant laws relating to a particular issue to be able to advice a client. The lawyer would also need to go through a series of questions in order to establish a client's case.

There can be uncertainty in the delivery and consumption of professional services. It is difficult for clients to trust the service provider since it is very difficult to evaluate the service during the search stage and even after the service experience. Clients depend on the track record and credentials of service providers to assess quality. The nature of professional services, also require high client contact –

Chapter Nine | John Kuada & Robert Hinson
Service Marketing in Ghana
London & Abuja, Adonis & Abbey Publishers and
Center for Sustainability and Enterprise Development (CSED)

i.e. the service provider and the clients spend long hours together in the service delivery process. This requires that the physical evidence of the service be attractive and comfortable to delight the client. The high contact service encounter also means that you must approach service delivery with the awareness that you do not have a second chance to make a good first impression.

Differentiating between professional services can be difficult. The services of two management consultants cannot easily be differentiated during the search and evaluation stages of service consumption. Potential service users can only evaluate the service after the encounter or the service experience.

9.3 Professional Services and Business-to-Business Marketing

Like in all other business-to-business marketing situations, there are three groups of factors that influence the buying process of professional services: (1) the marketing environment, (2) the type of customer (including the nature of its business), and (3) the composition of the decision-making unit within the customer company. The marketing environment in this regard covers government regulations, the economic climate within which the buyers operate, and the general technological changes within the economy. The nature of the customer's organisational structure, politics and culture also shape the manner in which purchase decisions are made. Finally, the decision-making unit (the buying centre) to which the purchasing task has been assigned also has a tremendous influence on the purchase process.

Thus, one can conceptualize the professional service purchase process by using the buy grid model. This model incorporates three types of buying situations and describes the different combinations of buying phases and buying situations. The three buying situations are as follows:

1. The new tasks situation,
2. The straight re-buy situation, and
3. The modified re-buy situation.

Chapter Nine | John Kuada & Robert Hinson
Service Marketing in Ghana
London & Abuja, Adonis & Abbey Publishers and
Center for Sustainability and Enterprise Development (CSED)

New Tasks Situation is a buying situation in which the business buyer purchases the service for the first time – i.e. novel purchase situation. In a new task buying situation, the buyer seeks a wide variety of information to explore alternative solutions to his purchasing problem. The greater the cost or perceived risks related to the purchase, the greater the need for information and the larger the number of participants in the decision making unit. This provides you as a service provider with considerable opportunity and challenges. You are in a greater position to influence the decision making process by the information that you provide the customer.

Modified Re-buy Situation is a buying situation in which your potential client wants to replace a service that it has been using. Take the example of a law firm that wants to improve its IT resources to maximize productivity and streamline operations to increase caseload capacity due to the influx of new clientele. It will ask a team within the firm to review the effectiveness of its current IT solutions redefine its needs, modify the service specifications and criteria for selecting service suppliers. The fact that the company had previous experience with the purchase and use of the service means that the decision criteria may be well defined in such situations. Nevertheless, some uncertainties may still linger in the minds of some decision-makers. The challenge you face in a modify re-buy situation is to convince your potential customer that by selecting you, the company will receive greater value than from the previous service provider.

Straight Re-buy Situation is a buying situation in which the customer routinely re-orders the service without any modification because the company is satisfied with your service offerings. But you need to be conscious of changes in your customers' needs or changes within the industry in which they operate so that you can suggest additions to the existing services you offer them. If you do not do so, there is the risk that a new service provider will offer them better conditions or draw their attention to some benefits that you do not provide them. If

Chapter Nine | John Kuada & Robert Hinson
Service Marketing in Ghana
London & Abuja, Adonis & Abbey Publishers and
Center for Sustainability and Enterprise Development (CSED)

94

that happens, your customers are likely to use the new offerings of your competitors to renegotiate your conditions of service offerings. Figure 9.1 provides an overview of the three buying situations and the decisional characteristics related to them.

Figure 9.1: Buun's Taxonomy of Buying Situational Characteristics and Purchase Behaviour

Decision Situational Characteristic	Purchase Situations and Behaviour					
	New Task		**Modified Rebuy**		**Straight Rebuy**	
	Strategic	Judgmental	Simple	Complex	Casual	Routine (LowPriority)
Degree of task Uncertainty	Moderate	High	Low	Low	Low	Moderate
Purchase importance	Very high	Very high	Quite high	Very high	Minor	Somewhat important
Extensiveness of choice set	Narrow	Very narrow	Narrow	Much choice	Very extensive	Much
Perceived Buyer power	Strong	Moderate	Moderate	Strong	Little or none	Moderate
Behavioural Profile	High level of info. search *Great deal of of analysis * No previous guidelines *Limited opportunity to control purchase process	Moderate amount of info. search, analysis and proactive focusing * No previous guidelines	Moderate amount of info. search and analysis * High level of proactive behaviour * Follow standard procedures	Seemingly rational behaviour * Great deal of info. search & analysis * Focus on long term needs and supply reliability * Closely follow established procedures	No info. search and analysis * No proactive behaviour	Limited info. search and analysis * Limited proactive behaviour * Follow standard rules and procedures

Adapted from Bunn (1993) p. 47

Chapter Nine | John Kuada & Robert Hinson
Service Marketing in Ghana
London & Abuja, Adonis & Abbey Publishers and
Center for Sustainability and Enterprise Development (CSED)

95

9.4 Phases in the Purchase Decision Process

Conventionally, business purchase decisions are expected to go through a set of phases. Purchases in new task situations go through eight phases, the number of phases and their relative importance decreases in the case of the other purchase situations.

Phase 1: Anticipation or Recognition of a Problem (Need)

In rational purchase situations, the purchase decision will be triggered by the buying organisation's recognition of a need, problem or potential opportunity to gain new benefits within the changing environment. The trigger may be either external (e.g. new information from a potential supplier), or internal (e.g. an awareness of declining efficiency due to outmoded technology and operating procedures). This is a phase in the purchase decision process during which the information a service provider provides is critical since the buyer is in wide search for solutions to the problem identified.

Phase 2: Determination of the Characteristics and Quality of the Needed Items.

Having acknowledged the problem, the next stage is to explore alternative solutions. It may be decided to solve the problem in a novel manner, i.e. exploring technical solutions unfamiliar with the buyer – (a new task situation). Alternatively, management may decide to find a modified/improved version of solutions with which they have been familiar – (a modified re-buy situation). Questions such as "what application requirements must be emphasised" and "what performance specifications should be used in evaluating incoming proposal" to receive attention at this phase. The department whose staffs are the users of the service will be prominent at this stage. Their suggestions receive serious attention. Prospective suppliers are, therefore, advised to examine the information needs of the users and provide it to them to enable them make the choices that favour their services.

Chapter Nine | John Kuada & Robert Hinson
Service Marketing in Ghana
London & Abuja, Adonis & Abbey Publishers and
Center for Sustainability and Enterprise Development (CSED)

Phase 3: Description of the Characteristics and Quality of the Needed Services & Phase

4: Search for and Qualification of Potential Sources

Having specified the characteristics that buyers should look for, the market is then scanned for the products that fit these characteristics and the quantities to buy. If a supplier has contributed information to the first phase, that supplier will be certainly consulted to advise the buyer on where to get the best products. If the supplier has the service in question, it is placed in a lucky position of influencing the choice decision. It may suggest modifications to its own services to fit the specific needs of the buyer. It has been shown that such partnering relationship with a buyer is highly advantageous in new task situations.

Phase 5: Acquisition and Analysis of Proposals

In this phase, qualified service providers are contacted with a request to make product offerings that can address the buyer's problem. In straight re-buy situations, the existing service provider will be the only supplier that the buyer will contact. For modified re-buy situations, there will be the need to analyse incoming proposals carefully before a final decision is made. The analysis of proposals becomes even more elaborate in new task situations.

Phase 6: Evaluation of Proposals and Selection of Suppliers

The decision-making unit carefully compares the various offers in terms of the criteria decided upon earlier. A few of the proposals are selected and the purchaser is authorised to initiate negotiations with the service providers concerned. Where the differences between the proposals are not significant, personal preferences and considerations indirectly enter the decision making process.

Chapter Nine | John Kuada & Robert Hinson
Service Marketing in Ghana
London & Abuja, Adonis & Abbey Publishers and
Center for Sustainability and Enterprise Development (CSED)

97

Phase 7: Selection of an Order Routine

Order is placed with the selected service provider and the delivery as well as payment conditions are specified. For some types of services, there may be a need for purchasing related machines and equipment. The purchase as well as the delivery, installation and training of users may be included in the contract. Here again the users' voice becomes very important since their evaluation is important in determining how successful the purchase has been.

Phase 8: Performance and Feedback Evaluation

This is the phase in which the performance of the product is matched against the expectations of the buyer in order to determine the gap, if there is any between them. As noted above, the evaluation of the users carries a heavy weight in the overall assessment of the performance of the service provider.

9.5 The Buying Centre Concept

Companies do not buy, people do. It is, therefore, important to have a substantial knowledge about those involved in the buying decision making process of the goods and/or services that a service provider intends to sell. It has been shown that many individuals are involved in B2B buying processes.

The theoretical foundation of the buying centre construct can be found in role theory. Role theory suggests that people behave with a set of norms or expectations that others have in the roles in which they have been placed. Roles can be both formal and informal. Formal roles are defined by organisational structure and managers' position within the structure. Apart from the formal roles that managers play, they (like all other people) have the natural tendency to develop informal social groupings within their organisations. These informal groupings can be harnessed to support the performance of the main tasks that have been assigned to them. Occasionally, however, some informal social relations can obstruct the performance of these tasks.

Chapter Nine | John Kuada & Robert Hinson
Service Marketing in Ghana
London & Abuja, Adonis & Abbey Publishers and
Center for Sustainability and Enterprise Development (CSED)

The Roles of Buying Centre Members

Buying managers are known to assume some common roles in a buying process. These roles are classified into six groups.

The **initiator** is one or group of individuals who become aware of a company problem and recognises that the problem can be solved via acquisition of a product or service.

The **gatekeepers** usually act as problem or product experts. They have information about a range of service provider offerings. Other buying centre members therefore rely on their information for their assessment of prospective service providers' offerings. Thus, by controlling information, and, by having access to decision-makers in the firm, the gatekeepers largely determine which service providers get the chance to sell.

Influencers have been described as those who have a say in whether a product or service should be bought or not. The more critical a purchase is to a company's business, the higher the number of influencers. Critically, strategic purchases frequently entail high resource outlays and affect the task performance of several employees the heads of whom naturally "have a say" in the purchase decision making process.

The deciders make the actual purchase decision. That is, they say yes or no to what service provider's offer. In less complex purchase situations, the decision-making responsibility may fall on one person. But where the purchase is complex, group decision may be required.

The purchaser is the one who makes arrangements for the delivery of the goods. He is also often directly involved in negotiating the conditions under which the transactions will be made.

The users are those who actually make use of the services in a normal working process.

Chapter Nine | John Kuada & Robert Hinson
Service Marketing in Ghana
London & Abuja, Adonis & Abbey Publishers and
Center for Sustainability and Enterprise Development (CSED)

99

A buying centre can be formalised, but not always so. Even in formalised buying centres, members are not designated with the titles of gatekeepers, influencers etc. A buying centre member may play more than one role at different stages in the buying process. There may be as few as one person playing all the six roles or as many as 50 or more in complex buying situations. The degrees of influence of these buying centre members will depend on their power base within the organisation.

One major characteristic of buying centres is that members come and go. The centre is, therefore, fragmented in terms of time, a phenomenon described in the literature as *time fragmentation.* The more buying centre members are involved for only short periods of time in the purchase decision making process, the more fragmented the buying centre is over time. This means that the influence of key buying centre members can be limited to a particular stage in the purchasing process. It is, therefore, of utmost importance to service providers to exert the best impact on them at the critical point in time to convince them of the superior value of their offerings.

9.6 Marketing Strategies for Professional Service Firms

Professional service firms need to project their unique competencies; skills and resources that set them apart from their competitors. Professional service firms must articulate their experience, superior skills, knowledge and qualifications of staff to portray how different they are in their area of operations, thus, instilling confidence in potential clients who will expect quality in the ultimate service delivery.

The strategies for professional service communications tend to sometimes differ from other services. This is because some professional service associations in the past restricted their members from promotional activities. These past developments have shaped the ways that professional service firms tend to communicate. Communication strategies for professional service firms should

Chapter Nine | John Kuada & Robert Hinson
Service Marketing in Ghana
London & Abuja, Adonis & Abbey Publishers and
Center for Sustainability and Enterprise Development (CSED)

usually be based on a clearly articulated marketing communication strategy. A marketing communication strategy usually describes in detail a market overview of the service sector in which a firm operates.

The development of company brochures, profiling of the company and the introduction the key personalities and their qualifications constitute a useful communication tool for professional service companies. The brochure serves as a mirror of the firm. It would provide all the necessary information on the firm to assist the potential buyer make informed projections of his service expectations.

Another means by which professional service firms can communicate effectively is to volunteer to make speeches at various fora. Such fora would include TV and radio discussion programmes, specially organized seminars in local business schools, Christmas (and other festive occasions) lunches and dinners for clients and prospective clients. These activities would make the service firm known and would give them exposure to captive audiences. African service firms can take advantage of such events to share their experiences and capabilities, thus generating goodwill towards their firm. In Ghana, some marketing practitioners, legal practitioners, investment bankers and medical practitioners have become popular and perceived as experts in their various technical fields because of their outspoken nature and their preparedness to comment on issues of national interest.

Professional service firms can also communicate through the use of organized seminars. For example, a management-consulting firm may decide to organize a seminar for a particular segment of the market and through that attract new clients who would meet them during the seminar. They would exchange information such as call cards at such a forum   and follow-up meetings can be scheduled for later. It is one of the opportunities for professional service providers to display excellence and competence in their chosen fields and to create a positive image in the minds of the audience.

Sponsorship of events such as tournaments and specialized walks

Chapter Nine | John Kuada & Robert Hinson
Service Marketing in Ghana
London & Abuja, Adonis & Abbey Publishers and
Center for Sustainability and Enterprise Development (CSED)

would also help to project the image of a professional service firm and create awareness about them. For example, clinics in Ghana can decide to organize a fund raising walk in support of HIV/AIDS patients. This would definitely come with some level of publicity, thus making them known.

Similarly, a law firm can also decide to take up free cases for minority groups in a community. This would make them known within the communities. The Centre for Public Interest law in Ghana undertakes such community cases free of charge and is given a lot of publicity in the media. An example of such a case was the ejection of the settlers at Sodom and Gomorrah, near the Odaw River.

Professional service firms can also volunteer to do media articles on regular basis to trade magazines. This would serve as a very good channel to attract the attention of potential users of their services. Their contribution would display their level of competence and serve as a point of reference for potential customers to evaluate them.

9.7 Summary and Action Points

Professional service marketing differs from other service marketing activities because it is usually between two organizations. The transactions are usually relatively fewer, but each transaction may be a significant share of your earnings. These transactions require close engagement with your employees spending long hours together in the service delivery process. It is also important to remember that many people in the client company are likely to influence the purchase decision and evaluation of the services offered; your employees' performance is constantly under the loop – closely watched by many experts.

To be successful as a manager of these processes, you must practice management by using the acronym of LEAD to the best of your ability. That is, you must be good at listening, engaging, authorizing your key employees to enable them take important

Chapter Nine | John Kuada & Robert Hinson
Service Marketing in Ghana
London & Abuja, Adonis & Abbey Publishers and
Center for Sustainability and Enterprise Development (CSED)

decisions on the spot, and **d**emonstrate expert knowledge about the services that your company delivers.

Chapter Nine | John Kuada & Robert Hinson
Service Marketing in Ghana
London & Abuja, Adonis & Abbey Publishers and
Center for Sustainability and Enterprise Development (CSED)

CHAPTER TEN

Concluding Lessons

10.1 Introduction

The previous nine chapters of the book have introduced you to the basic characteristics of services, the expectations of your customers and the manner in which they are likely to respond to your service offers. We have also provided you with some models for analysing the value of your customers to your company as well as tools for designing winning marketing strategies. The aim of this chapter is to bring together some of the main messages introduced in various chapters in a very succinct form and relate them to the experiences of some successful service companies and managers in Ghana. The experiences are presented in a general form in order not to expose the individuals and their companies.

10. 2 Ten Main Lessons

Lesson 1: Chose a Niche Market and Make Competition Irrelevant for a while

If you are contemplating on extending your portfolio of services it may be a good idea to reflect on Kim and Mauborgne's blue ocean concept. Their advice is that you must chose services that do not replicate those that many other companies are already offering. As they put it, "do not compete in existing market space instead you should create uncontested market space". Find a niche market – a place where you can fit and have an advantage over everyone else. You may not enjoy the advantage for ever. But you can use market position as a springboard to expand into other broader markets. You may do so by understanding the weaknesses of your competitors and the needs of their customers.

Chapter Ten | John Kuada & Robert Hinson
Service Marketing in Ghana
London & Abuja, Adonis & Abbey Publishers and
Center for Sustainability and Enterprise Development (CSED)

105

> ## Box 10.1
> Successful Ghanaian service providers are those that create something new and at the same time respond effectively to the declared needs of their customers.

Lesson 2: Pay Attention to your Qualifiers and Differentiators

The term "**qualifiers**" is used in marketing to refer to the core service that you offer. You must make sure that the standard of your services match those of your major competitors. We also referred to qualifiers as "Threshold or Basic (i.e. "must have") attributes" of your services (see chapter 2). Qualifiers are only noticed by the customer when they are absent or when they have failed. But in order to retain your customers and win new ones, you must have differentiators as well. **Differentiators** provide the customers with delight or excitement – you win the competitive game because of them. It is often said that small firms are in a greater position to compete with larger companies on customer service, because they usually have the flexibility to go the extra mile to make customers and potential customers feel valued. Make your organizations flexible enough to provide on-the-spot service differentiation with personal touch.

> ## Box 10.2
> You must exceed your customers' expectations, again and again – give them pleasant surprises frequently.

Lesson 3: Make your Key Customers the Ambassadors of your Company

Ambassadors serve as "door openers". That is, they serve as behind

Chapter Ten | John Kuada & Robert Hinson
Service Marketing in Ghana
London & Abuja, Adonis & Abbey Publishers and
Center for Sustainability and Enterprise Development (CSED)

the scene "workers" who generally leave a good impression about your company and make people curious to learn more. Studies have shown that customers that are very passionate about your services are likely to talk warmly about them. Their stories are likely to resonate well with potential customers since they will think of these stories as more trustworthy than the ones you tell about yourself. Even if your customers say pretty the same things as you do, their stories will have a tone of genuine passion behind them. In this way, your customers can open the doors to other potential customers' hearts more easily than you can.

Lesson 4: Leave a Good First Impression

It must be noted that all the efforts and investments that your company makes in order to attract customers will come to naught, if there is a negative first impression during a service encounter. It is, therefore, important for you to have a systematic means of developing courtesy among your staff at all levels of your company. You must also train your front line staff such as security personnel and front office executives to be knowledgeable and courteous in dealing with potential customers.

Box 10.3

You never get a second chance to create a first impression. Make it work the first time.

Lesson 5: Take Extra Care of your Regular Customers

Remember that the first step in getting your customers to like your company is to demonstrate that your company and employees like them. For them to succeed in their job, you must empower your frontline employees to be willing to take actions that will satisfy customers on the spot. No two customers are the same. Thus, employees should cultivate the mind-set that enables them to vary

Chapter Ten | John Kuada & Robert Hinson
Service Marketing in Ghana
London & Abuja, Adonis & Abbey Publishers and
Center for Sustainability and Enterprise Development (CSED)

107

their approaches to serving people. Be willing to replace failed strategies. If one approach does not work for you, if it brings repeated failure, then try something else. But you must develop rules and routines that reduce employees' anxieties about what to do in given situations. It is this combination of empowerment and guidelines that produces dynamic service delivery process in successful service companies.

Box 10.4

A successful Ghanaian service provider has this as a slogan for his
 Employees: "Behave today, as if this is the day you will be remembered by an important customer."

Lesson 6: Learn to Delegate and Relinquish Control

Empowering implies relinquishing some control. It is un-Ghanaian for managers to relinquish control. They believe that "it is safer to inspect than to expect". But a good leader must have the guts to relinquish some control and allow subordinates to make mistake and learn from it. All that you need to do is to make sure that your employees do not repeat a mistake – they build on their experiences.

But remember that not every link in your service delivery process will function effectively. Every organization has weak links. It is important for you to know your weak links and monitor those parts more closely than the other parts. Since empowerment of frontline service providers implies relinquishing control, make sure that you are close-by for consultation at the initial stages of the delegation of authority.

Being available for consultation means you are available to support your frontline employees when and where necessary – not to take over their functions. Your role must always be to help them develop their skill so that they will not need your presence next time.

Chapter Ten | John Kuada & Robert Hinson
Service Marketing in Ghana
London & Abuja, Adonis & Abbey Publishers and
Center for Sustainability and Enterprise Development (CSED)

Lesson 7: Always have a Back-up Plan

Successful business people always have stories of adversity in their bags. Things do not always go well in business life, no matter how well you plan and how well connected you are. You will always experience situations where Plan A does not seem to work the way you want it to or as fast as you want. So, it is always a good idea to have a backup plan (i.e. plan B, C and D) to fall back on. This lesson applies to all aspects of life, but it applies most particularly to service marketing due to the immediacy of "production and consumption" of services.

Lesson 8: Be a Good Listener

Encourage customers to complain and make it easy for them to do so. You must overcome the common customer perception that companies don't really care when things go wrong.

Berry, Parasuraman, and Zeithaml (1994) advise that "listening to customers and employees, keeping your ear to the ground, is the skill that makes service quality happens. If an organization cannot listen well, not much movement or development occurs".

They draw a distinction between "real" listening and "false" listening. To them "real listening" means hearing comments about your service and trying to appreciate the customer's point of view, even though you may not agree. False listening happens when organizations make pretence of listening solely for the purpose of obtaining support or buy-in without any intention of following through.

Lesson 9: Respond Quickly to Customer Queries

Companies often take too long to respond to unhappy customers, and then respond impersonally. By responding quickly, a firm conveys a sense of urgency. Quick response demonstrates that the customer's concern is the company's concern. By responding personally, with a telephone call or a visit, the firm creates an opportunity for dialogue

Chapter Ten | John Kuada & Robert Hinson
Service Marketing in Ghana
London & Abuja, Adonis & Abbey Publishers and
Center for Sustainability and Enterprise Development (CSED)

109

with the customer—an opportunity to listen, ask questions, explain, apologize, and provide an appropriate remedy.

Box 10.5

Be fair. Treat everyone the same, whether they spend 100 cedis or 1,000 cedis on your company's services.

Lesson 10: Learn to prioritize your time and those of others

It is often said that prioritizing in business can result in a 10% to 20% increase in the effectiveness of your resource usage. That is, you get 20% more out of your resources without any additional budget. This is very important for small service providers in Ghana – particularly those of you who have just started on your own. Prioritization will help you speed up your response time to your customers, thereby increasing their level of satisfaction.

Box 10.6

When you start your day's work, remind yourself of your goals for the day and identify the critical paths that lead to that goal; everything that is not on a critical path can be ignored or de-prioritized.

Chapter Ten | John Kuada & Robert Hinson
Service Marketing in Ghana
London & Abuja, Adonis & Abbey Publishers and
Center for Sustainability and Enterprise Development (CSED)

110

References

Assimeng, Max (1981) *Social Structure of Ghana* (Accra, Ghana Publishing Corporation)

Booms B. H. & Bitner B. J. (1980). Marketing Strategies and Organisation Structures for Service Firms. In Donnelly, J. & George W. R. (Eds.), *Marketing of Services*. American Marketing Association, 47-51.

Berry, Leonard L. Parasuraman, A. and Zeithaml, Valarie A. (1994) "Improving service quality in America: Lessons learned" *Academy of Management Executive*, Vol. 8 No. 2 pp. 32 -52

Daniel, Ebow (1993) *Ghanaians: A Sovereign People in Profile* (Accra, Asempa Publishers)

Day, G. S. (1999). *The Market Driven Organization* (New York: The Free Press).

Gummesson, E. (2002) *Total Relationship Marketing* 2nd Ed. Oxford: Butterworth-Heinemann.

Hofstede, G. (2001) *Culture's Consequences: Comparing Values, Behaviours, Institutions, and Organizations across Nations*, 2nd Ed, (Thousand Oaks, CA, Sage)

Kano, N., Seraku, N., Takahashi, F. and Tsuji, S. (1984), "Attractive Quality and Must-be Quality", The Journal of the Japanese Society for Quality Control, Vol. 14 No. 2, pp. 39-48.

Kano, N. (1995), "Upsizing the organization by attractive quality creation", Proceedings of the First World Congress for Total Quality Management, 10-12 April 1995, Sheffield, pp. 60-72

Kano, N. (2001), "Life Cycle and Creation of Attractive Quality", Proceedings from Quality Management and Organizational Development (QMOD), Linkoping University, Linkoping

Kuada, John (2008) *International Market Analysis – Theories and Methods* (London, Adonis & Abbey Publishers)

Kim, W. C. and Mauborgne, R. (2005), *Blue Ocean Strategy: How to Create Uncontested Market Space and Make the Competition Irrelevant*, Harvard Business School Press.

Chapter Ten | John Kuada & Robert Hinson
Service Marketing in Ghana
London & Abuja, Adonis & Abbey Publishers and
Center for Sustainability and Enterprise Development (CSED)

111

Kotler, P and Keller, K.L. (2012) *Marketing Management* Global Edition 14e (Boston: Pearson)

Lauterborn, B. (1990). New Marketing Litany: Four Ps Passé: C-Words Take Over. *Advertising Age*, 61(41), 26.

Martin, Beth Ann and Martin, James H. (2006) "Building a Market-Oriented Organizational Environment: An Implementation Framework for Small Organizations" *American Journal of Business* Vol. 20 No. 2 pp. 75-90

Matzler, K and Hinterhuber, H.H. (1998), "How to Make Product Development Projects More Successful by Integrating Kano's Model of Customer Satisfaction into Quality Function Deployment", Technovation, Vol. 18 No. 1, pp. 25-38 Parasuraman, A.,

Parasuraman, A., Zeithaml, V.A., and Berry, L.L. (1988), "SERVQUAL: A Multiple-Item Scale for Measuring Consumer Perceptions of Service Quality", Journal of Retailing, Vol.64 Spring, pp12-40.

Parasuraman, A., Zeithaml, V. A. & Berry, L. L. (1988). "SERVQUAL: a multiple-item scale for measuring consumer perceptions of service quality". *Journal of Retailing* 64 (Spring), 12-40.

Ryu, K. and Jang, S. (2008), "DINESCAPE: a scale for customers' perception of dining environment", *Journal of Foodservice Business Research*, Vol. 11, No., 1, pp. 2-22

Zeithaml, V.A., and Berry, L.L. (1985), "A conceptual model of Service Quality and Its Implications for Future Research", Journal of Marketing, Vol. 49 Fall, pp. 41-50

Zeithaml, Valarie A. and Bitner, Mary J. (2000), *Services Marketing (2nd Ed.)*, McGraw-Hill Companies Inc., New York.

Zeithaml, V.A. and Bitner, M.J. (2003), *Services Marketing: Integrating Customer Focus across the Firm*, 3rd ed., McGraw-Hill, New York, NY.

Chapter Ten | John Kuada & Robert Hinson
Service Marketing in Ghana
London & Abuja, Adonis & Abbey Publishers and
Center for Sustainability and Enterprise Development (CSED)

Index

Index | John Kuada & Robert Hinson
Service Marketing in Ghana
London & Abuja, Adonis & Abbey Publishers and
Center for Sustainability and Enterprise Development (CSED)

113

Index | John Kuada & Robert Hinson
Service Marketing in Ghana
London & Abuja, Adonis & Abbey Publishers and
Center for Sustainability and Enterprise Development (CSED)

114

www.ingramcontent.com/pod-product-compliance
Lightning Source LLC
Chambersburg PA
CBHW031813190326
41518CB00006B/317